Vegetables for Breakfast

Vegetables for Breakfast

from a to z

Change your breakfast, Change your life

Nancy Wolfson-Moche

Vegetables for Breakfast from A to Z
Change Your Breakfast, Change Your Life
by Nancy Wolfson-Moche

First published in the United States of America in 2020 by
Pomegranate Gallery Press, 137 Greene Street, New York, NY 10012

© 2020 Nancy Wolfson-Moche

With the support of Oded Halahmy Foundation for the Arts, Inc.

POMEGRANATE
G A L L E R Y
Oded Halahmy Foundation for the Arts, INC.

ISBN USA

978-0-578-68254-9

Text ©

Written by Nancy Wolfson-Moche
Photographs by Nancy Wolfson-Moche
Author's photographs by Jessie Adler
Book design by Yvette Lenhart LLC
Printing by Premier Graphics, Stratford, CT

First Edition. Pomegranate Gallery Press

youarebecauseyoueat.com/blog/

To my mother, Harriet Wolfson

TABLE OF CONTENTS

RECIPES

 FALL

WINTER

Everything we feed our body matters. Food spooned into the mouth, air inhaled through nose and mouth, sound penetrating ears, and ideas entering eyes, ears, nose and skin: all influence the cells that determine who we are. Every seven to ten years the cells replace themselves, and we are changed.

Cooking and eating are themselves transformative processes. Ingredients with various chemistries, textures and tastes merge to create something new and edible. We eat, and the body absorbs the nutrients and the energy of the food in its perpetual state of becoming. "Tell me what you eat, and I will tell you what you are," are the famous words of French lawyer and epicure Jean Anthelme Brillat-Savarin. The name of my business is *you are because you eat*.

As I write this in the spring of 2020, seeds are sown for a massive paradigm shift. We are called to change our habits and overhaul our lifestyle. This book invites you to open up to your potential to transform your being, breakfast by breakfast, meal by meal.

Breakfast frames your day, establishing its rhythm and tone. Reimagine your days as you reset your daily breakfast by adding a vegetable dish. In macrobiotics grains are whole, macro foods containing the plant's bran, germ and endosperm, while vegetables are micro foods consisting of one or more edible part of the plant. Start small, with the parts or details, by adding vegetables to your breakfast. Your condition will begin to change, which will spur changes in your life. Certainly.

THE BACK STORY

> *Eating is the transmutation of life from infinity. You are transmuting everything into your vitality, energy. This change is unlimited.*
> —MICHIO KUSHI

I created my blog and wrote this book to shake up your ideas about what breakfast can be. Changing my diet and lifestyle changed my life, and it can do the same for yours.

Several years ago I got married and wanted to have a child. I was over 40, and Western medicine classified me as being beyond childbearing age, so I wasn't eligible for high-tech intervention. Although it seemed painfully unfair at the time, this turned out to be a blessing. I was a freelance magazine writer at the time, so I approached my fertility quest as I would a story, pursuing every tip and trying each non-invasive modality I found, including acupuncture, Chinese herbs, prayer, yoga, qi gong, EMDR (rapid eye-movement therapy), shiatsu and macrobiotics. I began to sit down with my husband at regular times to home-cooked meals of whole grains, vegetables, plant proteins with small amounts of fish and fruit. It worked. On a 21-day trip around the world, somewhere

11

between Thimpu and Toledo, I conceived my first daughter. I am convinced it was the outcome of *all* of the various changes I made combined with my deep commitment and faith that I could do it. In addition to birthing my precious daughter, I lost 10 pounds without trying, overhauled my digestive system and became way more energetic with a heightened awareness and ability to focus. Six years later, I conceived my second child, another beautiful daughter.

At the time of my second daughter's birth I was coaching mostly women and families with a focus on fertility. I realized that the way to change the American food culture would be through children, so I began creating culinary arts curricula and teaching kids two years old and up to cook. They were excited about cooking and eating as they discovered the allure of delicious fresh food.

> One concerned for today plants grain; one concerned for the years to come plants trees; and one who is concerned for future generations educates people.
>
> — JANUSZ KORCZAK

BLOGGING

> *I feel a recipe is only a theme, which an intelligent cook can play each time with a variation.*
>
> —MADAME JEHANE BENOIT

Eventually I realized that to send the message to more people, I would need to do it digitally. A blog. It would be a blog. I asked myself which dietary or lifestyle modification had made the biggest difference in my condition and my life. The answer was, without question, the addition of a vegetable dish to my breakfast each morning. And so began my blog, *Vegetables for Breakfast* (youarebecauseyoueat.com/blog) in June of 2013. For one year almost daily I chronicled the vegetable dish I ate and fed my family for breakfast. When I was traveling, I posted what I ordered or bought in a store. One can always snag a raw carrot or a pickle. When the year was up in June of 2014 I continued blogging on a less regular, more monthly, seasonal basis. Often I post recipes and pictures of the whole breakfast, including the vegetable and grain dishes.

SERIOUSLY? VEGETABLES FOR BREAKFAST?

Breakfast. The word itself reveals its purpose. We wake up and break our "fast"—the longest phase during which we have abstained from eating within each 24-hour cycle. After its rest, our digestive system becomes active again. So the food we choose for breakfast must be designed to reawaken the digestive system with the reintroduction of food, gently. Gently.

Breakfast food should be gentle and easily digestible. After any fast, the first food introduced should be soft.

Breakfast kick-starts your day. It conditions your digestive system, letting it know what to expect as the day unfurls. If you eat it at the same time each day, between 6 and 8am, it propels your metabolism, conditioning your body to burn calories consistently throughout the day. Regular meal times reinforce this calorie-burning process. All vegetables contain dietary fiber. Soluble dietary fiber is essential for good digestion, so eating veggies in the morning promotes digestive health.

> *Be at least as interested in what goes on inside you as what happens outside. If you get the inside right, the outside will fall into place.*
> — ECKHART TOLLE

The heretofore Standard American Breakfast—a grain with something sweet combined with animal proteins like eggs and bacon—may have been the ticket for early Americans who led an active outdoor lifestyle. For most folks, those days are over. Now that most of us rack up a fair amount of screen time daily, our needs for beginning the day have changed. We need efficient, energizing, earth-based nourishment. Our virtual reach may be global, but our bodies must remain grounded and connected with our environment and our real-time zone. While we live with increased distractions that may challenge our time management, stress levels and digestive functions, our digestive system's needs are basically the same as they've always been.

It should contain a warm, soft whole grain in a porridge. Breakfast should be nutrient-dense, including a vegetable, like any of the vegetables highlighted in this book, and a plant protein like nuts, seeds, beans or bean products. It should contain almost all five flavors: sweet, sour, salty, spicy and bitter, providing a wide-spectrum, mainly savory flavor base for the palate. Start the day with a sweet breakfast and you prep your palate to expect more sweets, whereas if you set forth a range of flavors at breakfast, you will crave a flavor rainbow throughout the day.

> *Since we must eat to live, we might as well do it with both grace and gusto.*
> — M.F.K. FISHER

Upon hearing the phrase "vegetables for breakfast" many ask whether that is like eating dinner for breakfast, an idea endorsed by many a health coach. Well, no. The body's need to relax and tone down our energy at day's end is different from its desire for rising energy at breakfast.

So, how do we harness the rising morning energy on the plate? Cook for yourself and your family, always with love and positive intentions. Cook and eat fresh, locally grown seasonal vegetables whenever possible. Vary your vegetables from day to day and week to week. Vary the way you cook the vegetables, keeping in mind that the optimal cooking styles for breakfast are quick and simple: raw, blanched, steamed, quick-sautéed or quick-fried. Don't overcook them. Ever. The color of the raw vegetable should become more intense and vibrant when cooked. NO olive-drab or beige veggies for breakfast, please. We ingest more than just the data (vitamins, minerals, calories and fiber) of the food. We ingest the energetics of the plant: how and where it was planted and grown, with what it was nourished and the pace at which it thrived. Each ingredient has its own narrative that becomes a part of ours. *Chew* each mouthful *well*. Notice when you are 75 percent full, and stop eating. Be sure to leave some space for new experiences and ideas: don't head into your days too full of food.

"The tiniest movements affect our consciousness," says my teacher, Torah Yoga creator Diane Bloomfield. This holds true for eating too. Adding or eliminating one particular food, adjusting the quantities we eat, lengthening or shortening the time we spend supping, shifting the time of day we dine or adding a vegetable to breakfast every day can transform one's digestion, consciousness and very life.

> *More people will die from hit-or-miss eating than from hit-and-run driving.*
> — DUNCAN HINES

USE THIS BOOK!

This book invites you to eat vegetables for breakfast. Daily. The vegetable recipes constitute only part of the meal because... yes, there is more. A complete breakfast includes a whole grain and sometimes a plant-based protein dish. Each recipe includes suggested complementary grain dishes, and there are five grain recipes peppered throughout the vegetable recipes.

The icons accompanying each recipe indicate lots more info to up your food game.

> *I still think that one of the pleasantest of all emotions is to know that I, with my brain and my hands, have nourished my beloved few, that I have concocted a stew or a story, a rarity or a plain dish, to sustain them truly against the hungers of the world.*
> — M.F.K. FISHER

KEY TO THE ICONS

 Season – Ideal time of year to cook and eat the dish.

 Boom! – Time it takes to prepare the dish.

 How do – Cooking style used to make the dish.

 Eat this – Part(s) of this vegetable plant that is (are) edible.

 Go-With – Dish with which to pair the vegetable dish, usually a grain; porridge refers to any boiled cereal grain that is served soft and warm.

 Cook Ahead! – How to prep this dish before the morning you eat it.

 Lit! – Fun facts and tips about the featured vegetable including but not limited to its nutrients, the organs it strengthens, and conditions it supports along with little known lore and even a little dirt.

RECIPES

Asparagus Almondine

Serves 4

One bunch asparagus (about 10–12)

1 cup whole fresh raw almonds

¼ cup dried almonds (optional)

1 tablespoon EVOO (Extra Virgin Olive Oil)

Pinch sea salt

Juice of one lemon

Sometime between April and June, there is a six-week window when asparagus and fuzzy green almonds, still soft inside, are both ripe to harvest. Quick-sauté the asparagus to give it crisp, sizzling energy distinct from the firm-grape texture of the fresh almonds. Paired, they treat your taste buds to the unmistakable flavor of spring.

15 minutes

Quick-sauté

Shoot, bud

Barley risotto, brown rice, quinoa

1. Use a paring knife or peeler to remove the tough outermost layer of skin of the asparagus. Once peeled, wash them well.

2. Bias-cut each stalk into three equal pieces.

3. Use a paring knife to slit the sides of the green almonds lengthwise. Extract the soft fleshy almond inside, discarding the skin. Slice the flesh of each almond lengthwise, into 3–5 slices.

4. If using, dry-roast the dried almonds in a stainless steel skillet for about 2–3 minutes. Remove from pan and slice the almonds lengthwise.

5. Heat a cast iron or stainless steel skillet on a medium flame for about 3 minutes. Add the olive oil and allow it to heat for about one minute. Place the cut asparagus in the hot pan. As each side of each piece turns a warm golden brown (should take 2–3 minutes), remove it.

6. Place in a bowl and garnish with the fresh and roasted almonds. Squeeze the lemon juice on top.

asparagus

Asparagus is one of the few vegetables that is a perennial, coming up year after year. It is tenacious, needing to be planted only once every generation (25 years). Cleansing and a diuretic, it is rich in fiber, vitamins B12 and B9 (folate) and iron.

*Considered a vegetable Viagra since antiquity, asparagus was hailed by influencers including the Roman Pliny the Elder (1st century), the French Madame Pompadour (18th century), mentioned in **Apicius** (the oldest known Roman cookbook), the **Kama Sutra** (second century Sanskrit sex manual) and in **The Perfumed Garden**, a 12th century Arabic work of literary erotica.*

Sweet Beet

Serves 3

3 golden beets

Pinch coarse sea salt

½ cup raw pecans

1½ teaspoons pomegranate molasses (you may use pomegranate or date syrup)

1–2 tablespoons pomegranate seeds

These golden beets are peeled, boiled and served whole. When you eat the whole beet, its texture, color and mass are memorable. Eating this dish is a grounding, warming and, yes, sweet way to begin the day.

30 minutes

Boil

Root, leaf

Couscous, soft brown or red rice, porridge

You can boil the beets and roast the pecans the night before. Assemble and serve at room temperature in the morning.

1. Use a peeler to remove the tough outer skin of the beet.

2. Rinse the peeled beets and place them, whole, in a medium to large pot. Fill with water to cover the beets by at least two inches. Add a pinch of coarse sea salt and place on a medium to high flame.

3. When the water boils, cover the pot and simmer the beets for about 20 minutes, or until a fork easily pierces each beet. Remove the beets carefully from the water using a wire mesh skimmer.

4. While the beets are boiling, heat a stainless steel or cast-iron skillet on a medium flame for about 20 seconds. Add the raw pecans and use cooking chopsticks to continually turn the nuts so they roast on all sides. Note: they should be a light golden brown, not burnt. This should take about 3–5 minutes. Remove pecans from the pan and chop them into small pieces the size of pomegranate seeds.

5. Place the beets, whole, on a platter. Drizzle with pomegranate molasses. Sprinkle the pecans on top. Crown the top of a beet with a whole pecan or a pomegranate seed. Scatter a few pomegranate seeds around the beets and serve.

beet

Beets are among the least popular of vegetables, probably because of their earthy taste. A good source of folic acid, vitamin B-complex, manganese and potassium, beets are antioxidants, anti-inflammatory and may reduce blood pressure.

Ancient Romans were among the first to eat the beetroot. The rabbis of the Talmud (300–500 CE) recommended eating them for longevity. In the 19th century, the value of beets soared when they were recognized as a concentrated source of sugar. Sweet vegetables like beets, broccoli, cauliflower, onions and winter squash satisfy sweet cravings. Seriously.

Spicy Brussels Sprouts

Serves 2–4

8–10 Brussels sprouts, off the stalk

1 tablespoon EVOO

1 teaspoon whole brown mustard seeds

¼ teaspoon ground turmeric

1 shake cayenne pepper

¼ teaspoon medium grade sea salt

½ lemon

Whole or halved, boiled, roasted, sautéed or steamed, these mini-cabbages usually take at least 20 minutes to cook. Not these. By chopping them into tiny pieces and quick-sautéeing them in a sizzling hot pan, cooking time is a fraction of that. The tiny pieces disperse the tightly wound energy of this brassica, keeping all of its cholesterol-lowering, phytonutrient and vitamin-releasing potential intact.

15 minutes

Quick-sauté

Bud

Oatmeal, ojiya or rice porridge

1. Trim the ends and remove any brown or dry leaves from each Brussels sprout.

2. Wash them well by immersing them in water.

3. Slice each sprout into 4–5 thin rounds; cut each round into 4–5 vertical strips; chop each strip into tiny squares.

4. Heat a stainless steel or cast-iron skillet for one minute. Add the olive oil and mustard seeds. When the mustard seeds begin to pop, turn off the flame. Add the turmeric and cayenne pepper, and use a cooking chopstick to stir the spices together for 10 seconds. Move fast so you infuse the oil with the spices without burning them.

5. Add the chopped Brussels sprouts and salt to the pan. Turn the flame on and raise the heat to a high setting. Sauté the sprouts until they are crisp-tender, about 4–5 minutes. Taste and adjust the seasoning. Squeeze the juice of a half lemon on top (or to taste) and serve.

brussels sprout

Although cultivated in ancient Rome, they became so popular with the Belgians that they became known as "Brussels sprouts." They belong to the brassica family, which consists of 37 different species including cabbage, broccoli, collard greens, kale and kohlrabi. Brassicas are veggie royalty, as they are low in fat and high in vitamins, minerals, fiber and phytochemicals. Eat at least five servings of these beneficial vegetables each week. Super-rich in vitamins C and K and soluble dietary fiber, Brussels sprouts contain the phytochemical sulforaphane, which may prevent and fight cancer.

Carrot Flowers: Fried, not Baked!

Serves 4

2–3 carrots
3 tablespoons grapeseed oil
3–4 fresh mint leaves
Pinch sea salt

"Fried, not baked!" is macrobiotic teacher Denny Waxman's maxim. Many agree that fried food is tastier than baked food, but some may question its health benefits. Denny teaches that frying is beneficial when part of a low-fat diet; if you use (but don't reuse) good quality oil that can withstand high heat, fried food can be more nourishing than baked food. Baking vegetables will dry them out and eradicate some of the nutrients, while the heat surge from frying seals them in, giving the food a charge. Each of these artful carrot flowers is one-of-a-kind early morning eye candy.

10 minutes · Fry · Root, leaf · Millet mash, polenta, risotto

1. Trim the ends and scrape tiny hairs and brown spots from the surface of the carrots. Rinse them. Use a carrot sharpener peeler to shave paper-thin pieces that will form shapes like butterfly wings and flowers.

2. Wash the mint leaves and chop them into tiny pieces for garnish.

3. On a medium flame, heat a cast iron or stainless steel skillet for about 40 seconds. Add one tablespoon of the grape seed oil and allow it to heat up for about a minute. Drop the carrot pieces into the oil one at a time. Depending on the size of the piece, it will take about 10–20 seconds for the carrot flesh to turn a lighter shade and get brown around the edges. When it does, remove it from the pan and dredge on a brown paper bag.

4. Repeat this process until you've fried all the carrot pieces. Add more grape seed oil periodically, as the pan becomes dry.

5. Top the carrot flowers with the chopped mint and a pinch of sea salt, if desired. Serve them atop millet, polenta, risotto or any soft grain dish.

carrot

Carrots belong to the apiaceae family, along with parsley, fennel, cumin and dill. They are nutrient-dense, fiber-rich, high in phytonutrients (antioxidants) as well as potassium, vitamins A, C and K. Their alpha and beta-carotene may improve vision. Energetically, they are grounding and may encourage the eater to focus.

The first carrots, found in Afghanistan, were purple with woody, bitter roots, so only the aromatic leaves and seeds were eaten. In the 17th century orange carrots were cultivated in the Netherlands to match the color of the flag. Today, they may be white, yellow, orange, red, purple or black, depending on the soil, season in which they are planted, and weather conditions.

Cauliflower Rice with Corn

Serves 4–6

1 head organic cauliflower
(white, green, purple or yellow)

1–2 tablespoons EVOO

1 teaspoon sea salt or lemon
sea salt

1 cup fresh or frozen corn-off-
the-cob

1 teaspoon sumac (optional)

3 tablespoons pan-roasted
pumpkin seeds

Fresh-ground pepper to taste
(optional)

Cauliflower may be considered the tofu of vegetables because of its ability to highlight other ingredients and because it can take many shapes. This dish masquerades as porridge, with cauliflower assuming the size and texture of rice. While the sweet bitterness of this brassica may wake up your taste buds a tad faster than real rice, the dish's perfect balance of grain (corn), vegetable (cauliflower) and protein (pumpkin seeds) satisfies appetite and spirit.

40 minutes

Bake

Flower

Barley risotto,
couscous,
pita bread

Rice the cauliflower, toss it with the corn, olive oil and salt, and place it in the baking pan (steps 1–4), so it is oven-ready in the morning.

1. Preheat oven to 350°F. Line a baking pan or sheet with parchment paper.

2. Wash the cauliflower well by immersing it in a bowl of warm water with a splash of vinegar for about 10 minutes. Cut or tear it apart into smaller floret sections.

3. Use a Chef 'n Veggie Chop (shown here) or a food processor to mince the cauliflower into tiny grain-sized pieces. You may have to process it in two or three batches.

4. When the cauliflower is the size and texture of rice, transfer it to a large bowl. Add the corn. Stir in the oil and 1 teaspoon of lemon or regular sea salt until well combined. Place the moistened "rice" and corn in the prepared baking pan.

5. Bake for 15 minutes. Mix with a wooden spoon and return to oven for another 15 minutes, until the "rice" begins to turn a golden brown.

6. Garnish with dried sumac (a citrus-based Middle Eastern spice) and roasted pumpkin seeds. Serve warm or at room temperature.

cauliflower

"Cauliflower is nothing but cabbage with a college degree," said Mark Twain. They are cousins, both members of the brassica family. Right out of the ground cauliflower may have a bit more bling than cabbage, but in terms of health benefits, they are well-matched. One serving of cauliflower fulfills 77 percent of your body's daily vitamin C requirement, 20 percent of its vitamin K, 14 percent of folate and 11 percent of B6. It strengthens bones, supports colon health and may promote weight loss. Who says a vegetable has to be green to be beneficial?

Purple Daikon Corn Salad

Serves 4

1 purple (or white) daikon radish

8 grape tomatoes

2 stalks celery

2 ears corn

½ small spring onion (I used red)

1 lemon

1 tablespoon EVOO

1 tablespoon chopped cilantro (optional)

Sea salt flakes to taste

I find purple daikon at my local farmer's market. When I cut it open, the purple saturates the flesh as well as the skin. It is a tad more bitter than the more common white variety; you can make this salad with either. The bitterness balances the sweet local corn on the cob, whose harvest season is precious short here in the northeast. I added some local celery (for crunch), tomatoes (for juice) and a small red spring onion (for spice). The result: a crunchy, refreshing, rainbow-sweet way to meet the day.

15–20 minutes

Raw

Root, leaf, sprout

Barley risotto or barley salad (room temperature)

 You can cook the corn (step 1) the night or day before you make this salad.

1. Leave on the corn husks; trim the bottom off of each ear (to ease husk removal) and immerse in a pot of boiling water for 10–12 minutes, or until it smells corny. Remove from water and let cool.

2. Husk each ear. Shave the kernels off of each cob and place them in a medium-sized mixing bowl.

3. Wash the celery well. Trim the ends and any loose threads from the stalk. Slice diagonally, alternating directions. Pieces should be about an inch wide. Add to the bowl of corn.

4. Remove the tops and scrape the tough outer skin of the purple daikon. Wash well. Slice in half lengthwise; rest each half on the flat surface and cut thin half-moon shapes; then halve each half-moon. Add to the salad bowl.

5. Wash the tomatoes well. Halve them lengthwise; cut each half into thirds and add to the salad.

6. Cut a small red spring onion in half, lengthwise. Cut one half into half-moons and then chop each half-moon into small pieces; add to the mix.

7. Add chopped cilantro if using.

8. Squeeze the lemon and mix with olive oil. Drizzle over the salad. Add sea salt to taste, and mix well. Serve.

daikon

A mild winter Japanese radish, daikon is in the brassica family and is a strong antioxidant. Integral to Japanese cooking, daikon means "big root" in Japanese. Rich in vitamin C and low in calories, it strengthens kidneys and aids weight loss. Pulled down by the earth's gravity, daikon draws the deep, powerful energy from the earth and transfers it to the eater.

A key ingredient in Bangladeshi, Filipino, Indian, Korean, Pakistani and Vietnamese cuisine, daikon can be grated, boiled, pickled or cut-and-dried.

Six Shades of Green: Endive Fatoush

Serves 3–4

4–5 endive leaves

5–6 spinach leaves

5–6 sprigs watercress

1 scallion

5 mint leaves

5 sprigs parsley

1 tablespoon umeboshi plum vinegar

Greens come in a multitude of shades, visible in this fatoush, a salad of Arabic origin containing crushed seasonal vegetables and herbs. Endive is ivory to yellowish green, watercress and spinach are deep green, mint has a blue hue, while parsley is just a shade darker than grass. A scallion contains the whole range, beginning with white. Observe and munch mindfully on this medley of greens.

20 minutes

Raw

Leaf

Millet mash, steamed pita or sourdough bread

1. Wash the endive, spinach, watercress, mint and parlsey leaves, each separately. Rinse the scallion.

2. Chop the endive, spinach and watercress leaves, separately, in tiny quarter-inch-square pieces. Place them in a large glass mixing bowl. Chop the mint and parsley in similarly sized pieces and add to the mix.

3. Chop the scallion on the diagonal into thin ovals; chop each oval into tiny pieces; add to the mixing bowl.

4. Sprinkle the vinegar and toss all ingredients together. Serve on individual plates.

endive

Endive is a member of the chicory family, which includes bitter greens like escarole, frisée, radicchio and, um, chicory. Known as Belgian endive, this type has off-white center leaves that form a compact heart. It is grown in the dark to prevent its slim ivory to apple green leaves from turning bright green.

Rich in vitamin K, folate and manganese, endive nourishes bones and cells.

Fennel, Daikon & Shiitake Nishime

Serves 4

1 postage-stamp-sized piece
of kelp (kombu)

About 4 ounces fresh (or dried)
shiitake mushrooms

2–3 large round slices fennel

1 large daikon radish

3 dime-sized slices ginger root

Pinch coarse sea salt

About 1 tablespoon soy sauce

Nishime is a Japanese dish known to strengthen and cleanse, both attributes on my breakfast priority list. With just a quarter-inch of water and a tiny piece of kelp in the pot, vegetables steam for a half-hour or longer. They soften and sweeten so they are not only melt-in-the-mouth comforting but easy to digest. The fennel retains its licorice tang and the daikon loses some of its bitterness while the mushrooms remain woodsy.

40 minutes

Long-steam

Bulb, stalk,
leaf, seed

Millet mash,
sweet brown rice

You may cook this dish the day before. In the morning, remove from fridge and eat at room temperature. Or, place a scant ¼ cup of water in a small lidded pot, add desired portion of nishime, and reheat gently (on a low flame). Ready in 4–5 minutes.

1. Trim the stems from the shitake mushrooms; wash or brush them.

2. Wash the fennel bulb and slice the tough end off the bottom. Starting at the bottom, slice 3 pieces, each about ¼-inch thick.

3. Scrape any tiny hairs and brown spots from the daikon radish skin. Rinse it; then cut into 2-inch-wide segments.

4. Into a small heavy pot with a tight-fitting (preferably glass) lid, place about a quarter-inch of water and the kombu (kelp).

5. Arrange the shitake mushroom tops at the bottom of the pot. Layer the fennel discs on top of the mushrooms. Place the daikon radish logs at the top of the pot. Try to fit everything into the pot so it is tight and compact.

6. Peel the ginger root, slice it into disks and then into tiny matchsticks. Scatter the ginger pieces on top of the daikon.

7. Put the lid on the pot and place it on the stove on a medium flame. When you see steam coming out of the seams of the pot lid (after about 2–3 minutes) lower the flame to a simmer. Let the nishime cook for about 25 minutes, or until a fork glides effortlessly through the daikon.

(continued)

fennel

8. Remove pot lid and drizzle the soy sauce on top. Replace lid and shake the whole pot three times, decisively, with purpose. Return pot to a low simmer for about 3 minutes and then remove from flame. Arrange the nishime on individual plates, representing each ingredient on each plate. Serve warm.

Cousin to the carrot, fennel is a perennial herb used to flavor toothpaste, Italian sausage and the French liqueur absinthe. It originated in the Mediterranean and grew wild on roadsides. Until it became a favorite of Italian foodies in the 1960s, fennel was free foraged fare.

The bulb is rich in vitamin C, fiber and potassium, while the seeds also contain high amounts of B vitamins, manganese, iron, calcium and magnesium. It may strengthen the eyes and vision. Its powerful phytonutrients have antioxidant and anti-inflammatory effects. The high fiber content may reduce cholesterol and prevent colon cancer.

According to Greek myth, the gods presented knowledge to man at Mt. Olympus in a fennel stalk filled with coal.

Pair the vegetable dishes in this book with complementary grain recipes to make each breakfast seasonal, balanced, sustaining and delicious.

Serves 4

1 cup millet, rinsed

½ medium-sized cauliflower, washed and chopped (about 1 cup florets)

⅛ teaspoon sea salt

3½ cups water

Extra water for mashing

Fine sea salt, to taste

Fresh ground black pepper, to taste

A sweet-tasting gluten-free, protein-rich dish with the comfort and consistency of mashed potatoes.

30 minutes

Roast, boil, simmer

Carrot Flowers; Endive Fatoush; Fennel, Daikon & Shitake Nishime; Parsnip Curls; Winter Squash Nishime

You can roast the millet and/or chop the cauliflower (steps 1–2) the night before. Or cook the entire dish and reheat gently for about 5 minutes in the morning.

1. Lightly roast the millet in a skillet. Note: use no oil, just rinse the millet and put it in skillet on medium heat. Use chopsticks or a wooden spoon to continually turn the grain in the pan so it gets evenly toasted on all sides. This takes about 3–5 minutes.

2. Use a Chef'n VeggiChop to chop the cauliflower.

3. Bring the water to a boil in a medium pot. When water is boiling, add millet, cauliflower and sea salt. Cover and simmer on medium-low flame for about 25 minutes, checking to be sure it doesn't get too dry.

4. Mash by hand with a potato masher or purée in a food mill or blender, adding a little water if necessary to get consistency of mashed potatoes.

5. Taste. Adjust with salt and pepper. You may garnish with chopped herbs, toasted sesame seeds or a sea vegetable shake.

The Orange & the Green (Bean)

Serves 4

4–5 cups green beans
1 tablespoon EVOO
Pinch pink Himalayan sea salt
3 clementines

Also known as string beans, green beans are keepers, making them a good breakfast option pretty much year-round. They will last for five and sometimes even more days in your fridge. The best way to revive aging produce: chop it up into tiny pieces, put it in a sizzling pan to re-charge it, add something super fresh and polish it off. Check.

12 minutes

Quick-sauté

Pod, seed

Steel-cut or rolled oat porridge or polenta

1. Cut or break off dry, brown ends of the green beans. Cut away any brown spots. Wash the beans well. Chop them into ½-inch-long pieces.

2. Peel the clementines, removing the pith, and section them. Cut each section into 4–5 small pieces, about the same size as the green beans.

3. Heat a medium-sized stainless steel or cast-iron skillet on a medium flame for about one minute. Add the olive oil and when it is hot, add the green bean pieces.

4. Use cooking chopsticks or a wooden spoon to turn the beans, exposing all sides to the heat. When they begin to sizzle in the pan, add a pinch or two of sea salt. Continue to sauté the beans until they are bright green and coated with the olive oil, for about 4 minutes.

5. Remove from pan. Toss the green beans and clementine pieces together and serve.

green
bean

These beans are called "green" because they are picked while the pods are still green and the beans not yet fully mature. They are similar to snow peas because both pod and seeds are eaten, and different from legumes like pinto or kidney beans whose pods are discarded, beans dried and cooked. Many green beans contain a hard, fibrous strand that runs the length of the pod; hence they are also known as string beans. There is a stringless variety, first bred in 1894 by one Calvin Keeney, aka "the father of the stringless bean."

High in vitamin K, rich in antioxidant carotenoids, flavonoids and fiber, they also contain silicon, important for bone health.

Green Sashimi

Serves 2

4 ounces haricots verts
(thin string beans)

1 large carrot

Pinch of coarse sea salt

4 tablespoons soy sauce
or 4 tablespoons hummus,
for dipping

Sashimi is a Japanese delicacy composed of bite-sized pieces of tender raw fish artfully presented. Here, hold the raw fish, preserve the tender and the artful. Use a fresh carrot ribbon to wrap the tender haricots verts into a simple breakfast present. Each morning breakfast is a fresh, color-splashed, sacred gift.

15 minutes

Blanch

Pod, seed

Soft brown, black Japonica or white sushi rice

Blanch the haricots verts the night before (step 2).

1. Fill a medium-sized pot with water and a few pinches of coarse sea salt. While the water heats up, wash the haricots verts and the carrot. You may leave on the pointy ends of the haricots on to elongate the bundles.

2. When the water is rapidly boiling, add the haricots. When they float to the surface of the water and turn a more vivid shade of green, remove them with a wire mesh skimmer or slotted spoon. They should be done in about 2 minutes.

3. Use a peeler to peel the carrot so you have about 10 ribbon strips. If you peel it on one side, you will get wider ribbons.

4. Assemble the sashimi: on a wooden cutting board lay out a carrot ribbon. Bunch together about 7 haricots and place them perpendicular to the carrot ribbon. Tie the carrot ribbon around the mound of haricots. Repeat this until all the haricots are wrapped. Arrange on a plate and serve with soy sauce. For more plant protein, add a dollop of hummus for dipping.

5. Another option (bottom photo): You'll need two carrots. Blanch a carrot. When cool, cut it on a bias, slicing it into half-inch-thick oblong ovals. Use a carrot peeler to peel the other raw carrot, making ribbons as above. Place a ribbon on the surface; center an oval on top of it. Place one haricot on top. Bring the left and right sides of the ribbon together; tie loosely.

haricot vert

Rich in vitamins C and B5 and potassium, haricots verts contain more protein than many green vegetables.

In French "haricots" (pronounced "arr-ee-co") means "beans" and "verts" (pronounced "vair"), "green." In France, all green beans are called "haricots verts" and this younger, thinner, more flavorful and, yes, more expensive variety "haricots verts extra-fins." Haricots verts are a bit less fibrous than more mature green beans. Not your all-American dilly beans, haricots verts still make delicious pickles.

Italian Parsley Edamame Hummus

Serves 6–8

¾ cup shelled edamame
(or 1 cup in pods)

½ cup fresh chopped Italian
parsley plus additional
leaves for garnish

Scant ⅓ cup tahini

½ cup + 2 tablespoons
fresh-squeezed lemon juice
or to taste

2 cloves garlic

1 teaspoon fine sea salt

Freshly ground pepper
to taste

¼ teaspoon cumin (optional)

Drizzle of EVOO

¼ cup pine nuts

The tendency is to reimagine everything, even tried-and-true classics like cappuccino, chips, jelly beans and… hummus. Loosely defined, hummus is a protein-rich chickpea spread, made creamy with tahini (Middle Eastern sesame seed paste). In fact, "hummus" actually means "chickpea" in Arabic. Though it may be a misnomer, the spread is often as delicious and protein-rich when made with various beans like white beans and… edamame. Critical ingredient Italian parsley gives it a fresh, peppery, expansive charge to balance the compact density of the edamame. Did I mention this powerhouse plant is packed with vitamins and minerals?

30 minutes

Raw

Stem, leaf, seed

Corn or rice cakes;
steamed pita or
sourdough bread

Make the edamame hummus (steps 1–3) the day before.

1. Steam edamame for about 5 minutes until they are soft.

2. If in pods, shell the edamame and reserve ¼ cup of the beans for garnish. Place the rest in a blender or food processor with the tahini, garlic, lemon juice, salt, pepper, cumin (if using) and parsley.

3. Blend until smooth. If too thick, add lukewarm water, one tablespoon at a time.

4. Spread on thin corn cakes or bread and serve. Garnish with more Italian parsley.

5. You may also serve hummus with cut raw vegetables like carrots, celery or radish. Store leftover hummus in a tight-lidded container for up to 4 days.

italian
parsley

Herb or vegetable? Curly or flat? Italian parsley is an aromatic veggie. It is flat, and preferred by most chefs over the less flavorful, curly variety. Cousin of carrots and celery in the apiaceae family, botanically it is known as petroselinum crispum neapolitanum. Its thinner stems pack a lot of punch: chop 'em up and waste not.

Rich in calcium, flavonoids and vitamins A, C, B12 and K, it boosts the immune system, strengthens bones and can repair nerves. It is a breath freshener, a digestive aid and flushes out fluids, supporting the kidneys.

Ancient Greeks planted parsley on graves and Romans placed parsley wreaths near drunks for protection. It is used in purification baths by placing fresh parsley in a mesh bag.

Jerusalem Artichoke, Parsnip & Fennel Pancakes

Serves 4–5

1–2 large Jerusalem artichokes, aka sunchokes (about 1 cup, grated)

1 small- to medium-sized parsnip (about ⅓ cup, grated)

½ small fennel bulb (about ⅓ cup, grated)

1 scallion (about ¼ cup, chopped)

1 egg or 2 vegan chia eggs (2 tablespoons whole chia seeds in 6 tablespoons lukewarm water)

¼ cup spelt or gluten-free flour

½ teaspoon medium grade sea salt

Fresh-ground black pepper to taste

About ⅓ cup grape seed oil, plus more as needed

Several drops of soy sauce

Bitter greens or reds like trevisano or radicchio, or grated green apple for garnish

No maple syrup needed for these flapjacks. Made with three sweet and spicy roots and bulbs, these hotcakes are a riff on the classic latke. Served with fresh grated apple (for sweetness), and a leafy green or tangy, bitter red trevisano (above), this is a satisfying, sustaining breakfast dish.

 40 minutes

 Fry

 Tuber

 A pickle or sauerkraut

You can make the pancakes (steps 1–7) the night before and refrigerate. Fry them in the morning.

1. Clean the parsnip and Jerusalem artichoke by removing any dry, dark brown spots and tiny hairs from their skins. Wash both by immersing in water, separately.

2. Using a box grater, choose a medium-coarse grade and grate the parsnip.

3. Wash the grater and use the same grade to grate the Jerusalem artichoke.

4. Wash the grater and grate the fennel.

5. Remove the outer layers of skin from the scallion and wash. Chop the scallion into small pieces.

6. Use a medium-sized mixing bowl to whisk the egg or chia egg and sea salt together. Add the grated parsnip, sunchoke and fennel, chopped scallions and spelt or gluten-free flour. Mix well.

7. Fill a large soup spoon with the mixture and then use your hands to press it into a pancake shape. Form all of the mix into pancakes and set on a plate.

(continued)

jerusalem artichoke

j

8. Heat a large cast iron or stainless steel skillet on a medium flame for about 2 minutes. Add the grape seed oil. Place the pancakes in the skillet, leaving about an inch of space between them. When the pancakes are lightly browned on one side, flip them. They are ready when both sides are a golden brown. Dredge them on a brown paper bag (preferably without print).

9. Sprinkle one drop of soy sauce on each pancake and serve warm, with fresh grated apple or classic applesauce, with a bitter leafy green like watercress, radicchio or trevisano (shown on p. 42).

Jerusalem artichokes are also called sunchokes and sunroots. While these tubers have no connection with the city of Jerusalem, they do have a taste vaguely reminiscent of an artichoke. They are actually the tuber of a particular genus of sunflower. And the Italian word for sunflower is "girasole" which sounds like… you guessed it: Jerusalem!

Jerusalem artichoke is chock full of inulin, an indigestible starch that functions as a prebiotic, nourishing beneficial intestinal bacteria. These knobby tubers increase calcium absorption and suppress blood sugar levels so are recommended for diabetics.

To lengthen thy life, lessen thy meals.
—BENJAMIN FRANKLIN

*We never repent of having eaten
too little.*
—THOMAS JEFFERSON

Here, in the middle of a book of recipes, I suggest you pause to appreciate that the nourishment and energy you receive from breakfast is as closely connected with *how* you eat it as with its contents. Yes, it is essential to eat a vegetable and a whole grain for breakfast every morning. The following is equally as important.

The one item on every breakfast table in the world is a **hot drink**. It may be tea, coffee, hot chocolate, warm milk or warm juice. The temperature of the drink invites you to **sip it slowly**. I suggest drinking **green tea** with breakfast. It balances (being both relaxing and stimulating), contains antioxidants, refreshes the palate and heightens the pleasure of eating. Consider drinking **kukicha** (**twig tea** with an earthy taste that is believed to strengthen blood quality, soothe digestion and the mind); tangy **sencha**, smooth **bancha** or smoky **hojicha** (green leaf teas that lower blood pressure and blood sugar, promote longevity and may prevent and fight cancer); **genmaicha** (toasted brown rice with green leaf tea) or **matcha** (finely ground powder of carefully grown and processed green tea leaves). You may consider black or mushroom teas too.

Eat less. Two of our Founding Fathers said it (left) and author Michael Pollan reiterated it in recent years with this simple statement: "Eat food. Not too much. Mostly plants." Still, **we have become a nation of overeaters.** It begins with breakfast.

Carefully consider the size of the portion you wish to eat and that you think will satisfy all of your needs, including your desire not to overeat. Place the portion on your plate, mindful that this is your whole breakfast. No refills.

Breakfast whets your appetite for the day. **It prompts and provokes your palate, almost like a prophecy.** If your breakfast is sweet, you will crave sweets all day. If your breakfast is balanced and contains at least three of the five flavors, you'll lean into a range of flavors all day.

Give yourself the **time**: 15–20 minutes, **and space** you need for breakfast. **Sit down to eat.** When you sit, the digestive organs are angled to open and receive the bolus (chewed food) from the esophagus. **When you eat standing, the food does not enter your consciousness.** This is mindless munching.

Chew each mouthful **well** (for more on chewing, see p.59) and **savor every bite**. If you rush through breakfast, you're pacing yourself to rush through every activity that follows. Put less food on your fork or spoon and chew each mouthful thoroughly. You will eat less, digest easily and efficiently and feel satisfied. The more you chew, the less hungry you will feel during the morning and throughout the day.

Be grateful. My teacher Denny Waxman says giving thanks before and after a meal **wakes up the goodness in the food.** It will also open your heart, calm your belly and launch you into the day with a curious, decisive, compassionate spirit.

Kale, Chopped!

Serves 4

5–6 kale leaves (Winterbor is
used here; any variety will work)

⅓ cup pine nuts

1 lemon

¼ cup EVOO

Coarse or medium sea salt,
to taste

Freshly ground pepper, to taste

Leafy greens are a good strengthening way to start the day. They grow up and out, with expansive energy, which is generally the energy quality we seek to harness at breakfast. Yes, outward and upward is where we hope to head from the breakfast table. This simple kale salad sets us up to soar.

15 minutes

Raw

Leaf

*Corn on the cob,
polenta*

You can dry-roast the pine nuts (step 2) the night or day before.

1. Wash the kale well.

2. Dry roast the pine nuts in a cast iron or stainless steel skillet: heat the skillet on a medium flame for 30 seconds. Add the pine nuts and use cooking chopsticks to turn each nut, exposing each side to the heat. When nuts are lightly browned and smell lightly toasted (not burnt), remove them from the pan and set aside.

3. Use a knife to separate the tough spines from the kale leaves. Discard the spines.

4. Chop the leafy part of the kale into ¼-inch-wide strips. Grip the knife at both ends and chop the strips into small pieces.

5. Place the chopped kale in a bowl and add the sea salt. Use your hands to gently massage the kale leaves and salt together until the leaves soften a bit. Add the toasted pine nuts and pepper.

6. Squeeze the lemon into a small bowl. Whisk in the olive oil and pour over the salad, mixing it well. Serve.

Kale comes in a multitude of hues and over 50 varieties, with Winterbor (here), red Russian and lacinato (dinosaur) the most common and most available. Botanically speaking, kale is a brassica or crucifer in the mustard family. Crucifer means "cross-bearing" because of the configuration of the four petals of the mustard plant's flowers, reminiscent of a crucifix. Crucifer cousins include broccoli, cauliflower, Brussels sprouts and radish. Rich in vitamins C and K, iron and fiber, kale contains phytochemicals that can counter obesity, diabetes, heart disease, inflammation and cancer.

National Kale Day is celebrated the first Wednesday of each October.

kale

K

Green Pinwheels

Serves 2

1 8-inch-square lavash flatbread roll-up, cut in half

2–3 tablespoons of goat cheese, nut cheese or whipped tofu

About 14 small lettuce leaves– choose a mix of arugula, dandelion, gem, mizuna, mustard, oak leaf, upland and watercress, balancing texture, taste, color and crunch

The sandwich, universal hand-held-meal-in-one, was named not for the clever cook who invented it but rather for the Fourth Earl of Sandwich, John Montagu. He was a gambler who requested a simple utensil-free snack that he could scarf down without getting up from the gaming table. That was back in the 18th century. Since then, the sandwich has become the global 24/7 go-to meal. Not only portable, quick and satiating, it is whole, containing a grain, vegetable and protein. Eggless, this breakfast sandwich has all of those components.

7 minutes　　*Raw*　　*Leaf*　　*A celery, cucumber, carrot or radish pickle*

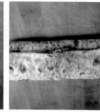

1. Fold and then cut the flatbread square in half. You will have two rectangles, each 4 x 8 in. Take one of the rectangles and lay it on a flat surface like a cutting board. Spread the tofu or cream cheese evenly on the bread, covering all of it. Place the assorted green leaves on top of the spread.

2. Turn the cutting board so the rectangle is situated lengthwise and roll it from the bottom up.

3. You will have a log-shaped cylinder. Eat it like this or slice the log into inch or half-inch-wide (bite-sized) pieces and arrange the colorful spirals on a plate. Repeat the process using the other half of the flatbread.

lettuce

1

Butterhead, bibb, gem, iceberg, oak, red leaf and romaine are just a few of the thousands of varieties of lettuce. Lettuce grows in heads, tightly closed (iceberg), loose (oak leaf), or as leaves on stems (arugula). A member of the daisy or aster (asteraceae) family, the darker the green hue and crunchier the leaf, the more vitamins and minerals therein. It contains vitamin A and potassium, with small amounts of vitamin C, calcium and fiber. It can be blanched, boiled, pickled, pressed or grilled. Lettuce's best assets? It refreshes, hydrates, cools and is crunchy.

First cultivated in ancient Egypt, it was used as a medicinal herb in ancient Greece and Rome. Thomas Jefferson was such a lettuce lover that he planted 15 different varieties at Monticello and ate lettuce dressed with egg, oil, salt, sugar, mustard and tarragon daily.

Water-Sautéed Mustard Greens with Sumac

Serves 3–4

1 bunch mustard greens
A pinch of coarse sea salt
2–3 tablespoons ground sumac
2 hard-boiled eggs (optional)

Mustard greens have a distinctly bitter, pungent peppery taste, and eating them cleanses the blood. Sumac, ground from the dried berry-like fruit of the sumac bush, has a sweet, citrusy taste. Sumac helps improve glycemic control (so it is a good choice for those with type 2 diabetes) and promotes cardiovascular health by inhibiting atherosclerosis (clogged, hardened arteries). While the greens are juicy, the spice is dry, complementing each other in color, taste, texture and purpose.

6 minutes

Water-sauté

Leaf, seed

Brown rice porridge or steamed sourdough bread

Boil the eggs (if using) the night before and refrigerate them.

1. If you are serving these greens with a hard-boiled egg (or half), peel the egg.

2. Wash the mustard greens well by completely immersing them in water. Drain. Remove the tough stems and chop the leaves into small strips about an inch wide.

3. Fill a medium to large skillet with one or two inches of water. Add the pinch of coarse sea salt and bring to a boil on a medium flame. When the water is vigorously boiling, add the greens. When they wilt and turn a brighter shade of green, they are done.

4. Remove greens with a wire mesh skimmer or slotted spoon, allowing the water to drain back into the pan. Arrange on individual plates.

5. If serving with hard-boiled eggs, slice the eggs lengthwise, and place atop or surrounding the greens.

6. Sprinkle a generous amount of sumac on the greens (and eggs, if using), letting it spatter on the plate.

mustard greens

Mustard, along with collards and turnip, is one of the traditional Southern soul food greens. Super-rich in vitamins K and A as well as calcium, mustard is a brassica with powerful phytonutrients that encourage the liver to cleanse the body of toxins. An anti-inflammatory that aids in digestion and absorption while boosting immune function, it is pretty much a magic bullet.

How these fringed green leaves are related to the spicy yellowish condiment in a jar: the spread is ground from the seeds of the plant, with added spices. In folklore, the mustard seed is often a symbol of a tiny, insignificant thing that grows into something strong and powerful. A German folktale instructs a bride to sew mustard seeds into the hem of her wedding dress to ensure that she's the boss. Danish and Indian lore encourage scattering mustard seeds outside one's home to ward off evil.

Napa Cabbage Roll-Ups

Serves 4–5

4 fresh large Napa cabbage leaves

1 beet

a few pinches coarse sea salt

optional condiments: peanut butter, tahini, umeboshi plum paste

soy sauce for dipping

You've gotta love a morning roll-up. Roll down the covers and roll out of bed. Roll up the covers and roll down to breakfast. Blanch, layer and roll these two vegetables, revealing their compatibility, flexibility and complementary hues. Infuse the day with these same sane aspects. Roll out the door and bring it on.

8 minutes

Blanch

Leaf

Soft brown rice or ojiya

Boil the beets (steps 2–3) the day before; refrigerate overnight.

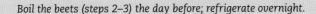

1. Wash the Napa cabbage leaves well, keeping them intact.

2. Peel the beet.

3. Bring two pots of water, one medium and one large (this can be a deep skillet), to a roiling boil. Add a pinch of coarse sea salt to each. Slice the beet into 4–5 quarter-inch-thick discs and place in the medium-sized pot. Lower flame and boil the beet for about 5 minutes, when a fork penetrates easily. Remove from pot with a wire mesh skimmer; set aside to cool.

4. Drop the Napa cabbage leaves into the large pot (or skillet) of boiling water, one at a time. Each will rise to the top in about 20–30 seconds. They will become a more intense shade of green. Remove from pot using a wire mesh skimmer, cool and set aside.

5. Slice the cooled beet discs into quarter-inch-wide logs.

6. Place a whole Napa cabbage leaf on a cutting board. Cut a small "V" in the bottom to make it easier to roll.

7. Place two of the beet logs on the cabbage leaf, about 1 ½ inches from the bottom.

(continued)

n

napa cabbage

8. Spread the condiment you choose (or none) on top of the beets. Begin to roll the leaf up, enwrapping the beet.

9. When you have rolled the leaf about three-quarters of the way, fold the outer green cabbage leaves in, covering the cylinder's ends. Continue rolling until it is a neat cylinder. Squeeze the finished roll, releasing excess water.

10. Cut the roll into ¾-inch-thick slices. Arrange on individual plates and serve with soy sauce for dipping.

napa cabbage

This is not another delicacy harvested in northern California's wine country. "Nappa" is the Japanese word for the leaves of any vegetable. This particular variety of leafy (rather than head) cabbage is also known as pe-tsai, celery cabbage, Chinese white cabbage, Peking cabbage, won bok, hakusai, pao and hsin.

Another member of the immune-system-boosting brassica family, Napa is low in calories, high in antioxidants, fiber, vitamin C and folate. It is an anti-inflammatory that can help lower cholesterol and, when raw or lightly cooked, protect against breast, colon and prostate cancer.

Napa is one of the cabbages used in kimchi, the super-spicy pickle that is Korea's national dish. Kimchi was traditionally stored underground in jars to keep it cool in the summer and to prevent it from freezing during the winter. Kimchi is included on UNESCO's Representative List of the Intangible Cultural Heritage of Humanity. Never underestimate the power of a pickle.

Pair the vegetable dishes in this book with complementary grain recipes to make each breakfast seasonal, balanced, sustaining and delicious.

Serves 3–5

2 cups leftover cooked brown rice or other grain (barley, millet, etc.)

1½ cups or more leftover miso soup

1¼ cups leftover cooked beans (use any bean, prepared any way)

1¼ cups fresh or frozen organic corn (optional)

1 umeboshi plum (whole)

1½ tablespoons sesame oil

½ cup black or tan dry-roasted sesame seeds for garnish

A Japanese porridge made from leftovers that is immune-boosting and super-strengthening.

Por' ridge. A soft food made by boiling the meal of grains or legumes in milk or water until thick.*

Porridge is the perfect breakfast food. Soft, warm, fibrous, easily digestible and nutrient-dense, it doesn't have to be oatmeal or the old classic Cream of Wheat. But it can be. This off-grid option goes well with many of the vegetable dishes in this book. Try it.

*Merriam-Webster

---

18 minutes

Gentle simmer

Baga Chips; Carrot Flowers; Fatoush; Napa Cabbage Roll-Ups; Parsnip Curls; Spicy Brussels Sprouts; Steamed Radish Roots & Greens; Yams 'n Sprouts

---

1. Place the brown rice (or grain) in a small pot.

2. Add the corn (if using). Add the beans.

3. Pour miso soup to cover grains and beans. Cover the pot.

4. Cook on a low flame for about 10 minutes.

5. Add the umeboshi plum (an antiviral and antibiotic) and cook for another 5 minutes.

6. Add sesame oil at the end. Serve garnished with dry-roasted sesame seeds.

Onions & Shitake on a Tofu Pad

Serves 1–2

1 yellow onion

8 small shitake mushrooms, fresh or dried

2 tablespoons EVOO

1 pinch sea salt

1 tablespoon sesame oil

2 squares firm small-batch tofu

A few drops of good quality, aged soy sauce

About ½ cup kale and/or dandelion greens, washed and chopped

Some mornings you need a little extra oomph. Try onions sautéed with shitake mushrooms, layered on tofu and topped with cleansing dandelion and strengthening kale. Mushrooms are classified as fungi, not vegetables. With filtering properties that support liver function, they contain vitamin D, not found in most other plant foods. Of the over 10,000 mushroom varieties, shitake has the highest percentage of D vitamins.

20 minutes

Sauté

Bulb

Brown or red rice

Grill the tofu the night before (step 6) and quickly reheat in the morning.

1. Cut the onion in half, lengthwise. Place the flat sides of the onion halves on the cutting board. Slice into them on an angle, cutting thin half-moons. Set aside.

2. Wash or brush the shitake mushrooms. I wash them when I buy them in an urban market; I don't want any city grime in my food. Many mycophiles (mushroom aficionados) don't wash mushrooms at all because the water removes more than grime—it removes the woody residue that gives the food that woodsy flavor. Your call.

3. Remove the stems. Slice the caps into small strips.

4. Heat a cast iron or stainless steel skillet on a medium flame for about 30 seconds. Add the olive oil and allow it to warm for another 20 seconds. Add the onions. Use cooking chopsticks to sauté the onions until they begin to wilt and sweat.

5. Add a few pinches of sea salt and then add the sliced shitake. Cook the mushrooms and onions together on a medium to low flame, allowing the flavors and textures to merge. When the shitake soften and are hard to distinguish from the onion, you know they are almost ready.

6. Heat another cast iron or stainless steel skillet (for about 30 seconds on a medium flame). Pour in the sesame oil and let it heat for 20 to 30 seconds more. Put the tofu squares into the pan; they should sizzle. When the edges of the tofu begin to turn a golden brown, flip them. Add a droplet of soy sauce onto each tofu square and continue to brown in the skillet.

7. When browned, remove with a spatula and place on a plate. Top with the mushrooms and onions mixture. You may toss the greens into the tofu skillet and quick-sauté or blister them. Otherwise, leave them raw. Layer the greens on top of the shitake-onion sauté. Serve.

(continued)

onion

onion

Onion is an allium, like chive, garlic, leek, scallion and shallot. Anti-inflammatory, antibacterial and cholesterol-lowering, onions are 89 percent water, with small amounts of fiber, B and C vitamins and protein.

Red, white or yellow, onions were used as medicine in ancient cultures. They've cured headaches, coughs, flu, hair loss and snakebites. Many holistic doctors suggest rubbing them on insect bites. Although mouth-puckeringly spicy when eaten raw, onions become sweet when cooked.

Egyptian art is partial to the humble onion; it is represented more often than any other vegetable. There's been lots of chatter about the jewels and honey ancient Egyptians took with them to the tomb. Add onions to the list: it was thought the smell could restore life to the dead. Roman gladiators were rubbed down with onions to strengthen their muscles, and in the Middle Ages onions were used as currency.

If you truly get in touch with a piece of carrot, you get in touch with the soil, the rain, the sunshine. You get in touch with Mother Earth and eating in such a way, you feel in touch with true life, your roots, and that is meditation. If we chew every morsel of our food in that way we become grateful and when you are grateful, you are happy.

—THICH NHAT HANH

I do not drink smoothies. Why? Although you may receive some of the benefits of the fruits and veggies in the drink, **you don't get to chew it.** And chewing is one of the most important facets of eating any meal, and breakfast in particular.

Digestion begins in the mouth, where the teeth function like the options on your blender: they chop, grind, blend and purée. When food enters the mouth, it meets saliva that contains digestive enzymes. This moment of meeting is when the digestive breakdown begins. The more you chew, the more digestive enzymes you produce, initiating smoother, more efficient, more complete digestion. You will notice a change immediately.

In addition to kicking off the digestive process, **chewing takes time**, giving your system another edge. It gives the brain time to receive the news from the digestive organs letting it know you are full. Unfortunately, we've become accustomed to eating faster than it takes the brain to get the ALL FULL memo, until it is too late and we have already overeaten. So the more you chew, the sooner you'll feel full, the less you'll eat, the smoother the digestive process will go, the more effectively you will metabolize your food and the less weight you will gain. If you want **to lose pounds, make no change in your diet other than chewing** each mouthful 30–50 times, and prepare to have your socks, er, pounds, knocked off. I promise.

Chewing well gives you an opportunity to really **taste the food.** The longer food remains in your mouth, the more time the brain has to receive messages from its thousands of taste receptor cells (aka taste buds). Have you ever tried chewing a pretzel 50 times? With the first 10 chews, you taste the yummy salty crunchiness. After the next 10 chews, you begin to notice the overwhelmingly bland floury taste. By the 30th chew, you begin

to realize that the pretzel is super-dry, like cardboard. The same is true of many packaged snacks. Try chewing your favorites 30–50 times, and watch your cravings wane.

On the other hand, try chewing a snap pea or sprig of parsley 50 times. The longer you chew, the more of the **pure, earthy flavor releases in your mouth**, intensifying with each chomp. Chewing encourages appreciation of fresh, local produce and of simple, carefully cooked dishes.

Practically speaking, chewing well prevents choking. It also encourages you to chew ideas thoroughly. Swishing the food from side to side, noticing how the texture transforms, is a paradigm for how you will collect and process ideas.

59

CHEW! · Cultivate Chewing

When walking, walk. When eating, eat.
— ZEN PROVERB

- Put a small amount of food on your fork or spoon.

- Once the food is in your mouth, rest your fork or spoon back on the plate.

- Focus your attention and all five senses on the food and chewing.

- It's best not to talk and chew at the same time.

- Do not read, talk or handle any electronic device while you chew.

If you chew well, you can think better. If you have a difficult problem, chew very well. Then you can always find a solution.

—HERMAN AIHARA

1. Sit in a chair, with legs uncrossed and **feet grounded** on the floor. This maximizes the position of the digestive organs so the digestive process will work most efficiently. Alternatively, you may sit on the floor in a comfortable position in which legs are not crossed and feet touch the ground (kneeling in seiza position).

2. **Lengthen your spine**, thinking of stacking the vertebrae, one on top of the other, from the sacrum to the occipital bone.

3. **Relax** your **shoulders**, drawing them back and down.

4. **Relax** your **neck**.

5. **Drop your chin** slightly—this maximizes spine extension and **turns the focus inward**. It is the best posture for chewing, because it doesn't send the food right down the hatch. It keeps the food in the front of the mouth, giving you the opportunity to chew longer.

6. Put a raisin or dried cranberry in the **front of your mouth** and begin to chew. Try to keep the raisin in the front of your mouth as you move it from one side of the mouth to the other, and back again. Remain silent. Count each chew, and try to reach at least 30. Aim to reach 50. Eventually, once you have a sense of what 30–50 chews feels like, it may be unnecessary and more relaxing not to count.

7. When there is nothing left in your mouth, **taste** what remains on your tongue. **Listen** to your body, to your digestive organs. Taste your digestive juices. **Appreciate** that you used **all five senses** in this exercise: you SAW, you TOUCHED, you SMELLED, you HEARD, and you TASTED the food.

In Japanese there are two words for thinking: one for casual thinking and one for deep thinking. The word for chewing and deep thinking is the same.

—DENNY WAXMAN

Parsnip Curls

Serves 3

2–3 parsnips

1 tablespoon grape seed oil

Drizzle of EVOO

A few pinches coarse or medium sea salt

This eye candy is short on cooking time and long on sweet crunch. As the temperature dips, the body needs foods rich in nutrients and fats. Parsnips—harvested in most climes after the first frost to maximize sweetness—fill the bill. Because they are super-fibrous and flavorfully complex, parsnips are usually long-cooked. Peeling and baking them makes for a quick-to-prepare breakfast dish. You eat the flesh closest to the skin where most of the flavor resides, so you get the best of this root veg. Win-win.

17 minutes

Bake

Root

Barley risotto, millet mash, ojiya or polenta

1. Preheat oven to 375°F. Trim the tops and bottoms of parsnips. Scrub the outer layer of parsnip skin; do not peel it as the strongest flavor resides right under the skin. Use a peeler to shave the top layers of the parsnip. Continue to shave the same spot so the peel becomes thicker. When close to the core, turn the parsnip and shave the opposite side. Continue peeling all four sides. You should have several wide strips about 4 inches long, or the length of the parsnip.

2. Roll them up, starting with the wider side of the strip.

3. Lay them in a baking or roasting dish. They will shrink a bit.

4. Drizzle the grape seed oil evenly over all the curls. Sprinkle with sea salt.

5. Bake for about 10 minutes. It may take more or less than 10; that will depend on the density of the parsnips, and on the oven. Check them after 7–8 minutes. When the edges are lightly browned, but not burnt, they are done. Drizzle sparingly with olive oil and serve.

parsnip

A close relative of both carrot and parsley, this root takes a long time to mature. In the northeast, seeds sown in early spring are harvested after the first frost. The frost forces the parsnip to convert starch into sugar as a natural defense mechanism to prevent cell damage from the cold. This extended time underground gives parsnips extra strengthening properties.

Super-rich in potassium, dietary fiber, folate and vitamin C, parsnips contain antioxidants with antifungal, anti-inflammatory and anti-cancer properties.

Once a dietary staple of the poor in Europe and England, the parsnip was brought by colonists to North America. It became America's winter root-vegetable-of-choice until it was usurped by the humble white potato, which is actually not a root but a tuber.

Quinoa Tabouleh

Serves 4

1 cup quinoa

About 1 teaspoon sea salt

1 large bunch flat-leaf parsley

2 large or 3 medium-sized tomatoes

2–3 Persian cucumbers

4–6 sprigs fresh mint

4–5 scallions

2 lemons

2 tablespoons EVOO

A few edible flowers (here, tricolor viola) and lettuce for garnish

Quinoa is more vegetable than grain. It is the seed of a plant that more closely resembles spinach than any grass or cereal grain. This gluten-free dish subs quinoa for bulgur wheat, the cracked grain commonly used to make Middle Eastern tabouleh. An authentic tabouleh should contain at least as many specks of chopped parsley as tiny grain kernels.

Seeds are all about possibility. Within each seed lies the potential to grow into something vital that might improve the world. Another thing about seeds: they are patient, waiting until the moment is ripe for their growth and expansion. When we eat seeds, we are absorbing their potential. And isn't breakfast all about harnessing our own potential for the day ahead?

40 minutes (15–20 if quinoa is pre-cooked)   Boil   Seed   A bed of cooked or raw greens

Cook the quinoa (step 2)—or prepare the whole dish—the night or day before, and store it in the fridge.

1. Quinoa must be washed thoroughly at least three times to prevent it from tasting bitter. The bitterness comes from saponin, a natural soapy-tasting chemical that coats each quinoa seed to protect the plant from predators.

2. Wash the quinoa well by immersing in a bowl of cold water, letting it sit for 5 minutes or more, and then agitating and rinsing well. The water will look bubbly and sudsy. Repeat this three times. Into a medium-sized pot pour 4 cups water. Add a pinch of sea salt and bring to a boil. Add the washed quinoa and allow water to boil again; lower the heat to a simmer and cover the pot. Cook for about 30 minutes, until all water is absorbed and quinoa is still moist. Allow quinoa to sit for about 10 minutes and then transfer it to a glass or ceramic bowl and allow to cool.

3. While the quinoa cooks, chop the parsley, cucumber, tomatoes, scallions and mint into tiny pieces and set aside.

4. When the quinoa is cool, add a small amount (about one-fifth) to a large glass or ceramic bowl. Layer the quinoa, parsley, cucumber, tomatoes, scallions and mint. Repeat this 4–5 times, then mix all layers together.

quinoa

q

(continued)

65

5. Pour the lemon juice, drizzle the olive oil and season with sea salt. Mix it all up well.

6. Garnish with lettuce greens and edible flowers. Serve.

7. Stored in a covered glass jar or container in the fridge, quinoa tabouleh will keep for up to three days.

Quinoa is a member of the Chenopodiaceae plant family with spinach, Swiss chard and beets. It grows high in the Andes mountains of Peru and Bolivia and the Rockies of the United States where the soil is thin and rain scarce, an unlikely spot for anything to thrive. If the plant can grow in such adverse conditions, it has to be strong and hardy. Eating it transmits these qualities to the body.

This seed packs a lot of punch. The tiny seed expands up to four times in size when cooked. As it cooks, the germ separates from the kernel, appearing as a little white halo, an indication that it is fully cooked. Rich in iron, high in monounsaturated fats (the good fats) and low in carbs, quinoa contains all 9 amino acids, making it a complete plant protein.

Quinoa was sacred to the Incas, who named it the Mother Grain. The Incan emperor ceremoniously sowed the first quinoa seeds of the season using tools of solid gold.

Salt has a greater impact on flavor than any other ingredient. Learn to use it well, and your food will taste good.

—SAMIN NOSRAT

Salt is a mineral that is an important condiment in every pantry. It draws out flavor, amplifies, balances, enhances and preserves.

It can speed up the time it takes to cook vegetables. It is important to use good quality, carefully sourced sea salt. Like table salt, it is made of sodium chloride, but **sea salt contains additional trace minerals like potassium, iron and zinc.** Both sodium and chloride are vital for our health, in very small amounts. Sea salt is harvested after the simple evaporation of seawater, whereas table or rock salt is mined from the salt deposits in ancient seas and lakes.

Microplastics have been detected in many salts, so choose your salt with care and information. Sea salt comes from the sea, and all water on our planet is affected by climate change, so keep this in mind. **Note where the salt is harvested, by whom and whether it has been checked for microplastics and other environmental toxins.**

It is best to have on hand four grades of sea salt: coarse (aka kosher salt), medium, fine and flakes.

Coarse or kosher salt is used for pickling, roasting and for boiling water when boiling or blanching vegetables. **Medium** is my preferred salt for cooking vegetable dishes, particularly steaming, sautéeing, and most stove-top cooking. **Fine** salt is used for baking muffins or cake. **Flakes**, with their dry, noticeably flat crystals, are a finishing salt, adding flavor, crunch and bling. Salt flakes are sprinkled mindfully onto a dish right before serving. Flakes are a pantry extra rather than a necessity.

The more you eat, the less flavor; the less you eat, the more flavor.

—CHINESE PROVERB

But don't forget that memory is like salt: the right amount brings out the flavour in food, too much ruins it. If you live in the past all the time, you'll find yourself with no present to remember.

—PAULO COELHO

SALT SELECTS

All grades
Kalustyan, New York City
kalustyans.com

Saltworks
seasalt.com

Fine
Masu salt
naturalimport.com

Medium
SI sea salt
healthgoods.com

Trapani sea salt
eataly.com
or dolceterra.com

Coarse (Kosher)
Maine sea salt (coarse grain)
foodsofnations.com

Sal Real de Colima
avajaneskitchen.com
or amazon.com

Flakes
Maldon sea salt flakes
amazon.com

Steamed Radish Roots & Greens

Serves 2–4

1 bunch fresh pink radishes, including tops

4–8 drops good-quality aged soy sauce

We all seek balance. One way to achieve a balanced condition is to eat foods that are balanced. The part of the radish we are accustomed to eating is the root, which is grounding and has contractive energy. The leafy greens have expansive, upward-reaching energy and are especially delicious when cooked with the roots. Eating roots and tops for breakfast begets a balanced beginning of your day. Steaming is the cooking style that allows for best retention of vitamins in vegetables.

8 minutes

Steam

Root, leaf and oil from seed

Fried rice, ojiya, pancakes or polenta

1. Wash the radish roots and greens well. Separate the roots from the greens. Remove any tough spots on each radish.

2. Cut each radish in half, lengthwise. Cut it into quarters or sixths.

3. Chop the leaves into small pieces by cutting them into quarter-inch-thick sections and chopping those into smaller pieces.

4. Add 1–2 inches of water to a steamer pot; bring water to a boil. Place radish roots on the bottom and greens on top in the steamer basket.

5. Place the steamer basket into the pot and cover. Steam the roots and greens until the greens are wilted. This should take 2–4 minutes.

6. Add a few drops of soy sauce while they are still in the basket.

7. Arrange the roots and greens on individual plates and serve.

radish

These peppery-flavored brassicas (cousins of mustard, cabbage and turnip) get their tang from various naturally occurring chemical compounds produced by the plants.

Radishes are fast-growing (about 21 days from seed to table) appetite stimulants and immune system boosters, nourishing us with vitamin C. Bitter receptors line the digestive tract; when activated by bitter foods like radishes they stimulate the immune system, warding off infection.

The Romans ate bread and relish for breakfast daily, and the relish was often made with radish.

Remember that quintessential garden crasher, Peter Rabbit? He was eating long scarlet radishes, not carrots. His creator, Beatrix Potter, herself a gardener, knew how much rabbits love radishes. Bugs Bunny and the carrots? A cartoon.

Baga Chips

Serves 4

1 rutabaga

¼ cup grapeseed oil, more as needed

A few pinches sea salt flakes, like Maldon, to taste

Rutabaga is a root in search of its culinary identity. It has been called the new kale and a Swedish turnip (I've been called worse). Prior to 1980 various regions in the United Kingdom had the tradition of carving rutabagas into lanterns for Halloween. I use it as a potato proxy in creamy creamless soups and in these chips because it surpasses the white potato in nutrients and health benefits. These rutabaga (aka "baga") chips are a riff on the classic breakfast hash browns.

15 minutes

Fry

Root, leaf

Oatmeal, ojiya, risotto or soft rice

1. Use a paring knife to remove any little hairs or rough spots from the skin of the rutabaga. Wash it well. Cut it in half, lengthwise (slicing it through the bottom point and the wider, hard flat top).

2. Place one half on a cutting board, flat side down. Starting at the bottom, slice into the rutabaga on the diagonal, creating thin oblong crescent shapes.

3. Finish slicing both halves. Set the crescents aside. Heat a cast iron or stainless steel skillet for about 2 minutes. Add about 3 tablespoons grapeseed oil. Carefully drop the rutabaga crescents into the oil until they fill the bottom layer of the pan. When they begin to brown around the edges, use wooden tongs to turn each one over.

4. When both sides are slightly browned, remove from pan and dredge on a brown paper bag (make sure it is not printed with colored dyes).

5. When much of the oil has seeped out, serve, topped with a sprinkle of sea salt flakes.

rutabaga

This cabbage-turnip hybrid was probably first cultivated in the late Middle Ages. It is a brassica that can be baked, boiled, roasted, mashed or fried. Some people even eat them raw, julienned. Rich in potassium, phosphorus, folate, vitamin C and magnesium, rutabaga has many of the benefits of a turnip minus a tad of its bitterness.

It is inexpensive and winters over, so it has been appreciated in times of war, food shortage and famine. Many World War II survivors describe rutabaga soup as a staple in those years. This savior vegetable merits a Rutabaga Renaissance.

Yellow Carrot Nori Rolls

Serves 2–3

2 yellow carrots
3 half-sheets toasted nori
Soy sauce for dipping
6 red raspberries

Think about it. Sea vegetables grow in water rather than in dirt. They are a vital vegetable, providing us with minerals unique to the ocean with its incomparable energy and strength. Once the domain of Japanese and other Asian cuisines, nori is now a ubiquitous global sea vegetable. It is used to make sushi, which has become the new sandwich. Like the sandwich, sushi is portable finger-food that travels well. Like the sandwich, it is a whole meal, supplying a grain, a vegetable and a protein. This nori roll is a simple breakfast option, minus the grain. Have the rice on the side and trust that the nori and rice have your breakfast protein needs covered.

7 minutes

Dried and toasted

Leaf

White, brown, green (jade pearl or bamboo-infused) or red rice

1. Wash the carrots well. Remove tiny hairs and dark spots.

2. Slice the carrot into oblong ovals. Cut the ovals, lengthwise, into thin matchsticks.

3. Have a small finger bowl of water nearby (water will hold the nori together). Place the half-sheet of nori on a sushi mat, shiny side facing down, matte side up. Line up the bottom of the nori sheet with the bottom of the sushi mat. Place the carrot matchsticks horizontally about 2 inches from the bottom of the nori.

4. Dip your forefinger into the water bowl and slide it along the bottom of the nori, as if moistening an envelope. Don't use too much water or the nori will get soggy. Once moistened, fold the nori over the carrots and secure it to the other side of the nori sheet.

5. Move the whole roll back to the base of the sushi mat and moisten the far side of the nori sheet with your finger. Roll it up, inside the mat, squeezing the mat so the nori is rolled tightly. Remove the mat and slice the roll into two or three pieces.

6. Garnish with fresh raspberries and serve with soy sauce for dipping.

sea
vegetable

S

Also known as laver, nori is a red algae whose biological name is pyropia. Other common edible sea vegetables are arame, dulse, hijiki, kombu or kelp and wakame.

Sea vegetables contain trace minerals not found in other foods. They are super-rich in iodine, providing more of it than any other food. They are a source of vitamins A, B, C, E and K, as well as bio-available iron, potassium, selenium, calcium and iron. Sea veggies may prevent and fight cancer, promote detoxification and help stimulate hair growth.

Although nori has been eaten in Japan since ancient times, the first record of it as a common food is in the 8th century, when it was enjoyed as a paste or condiment. The sheet form was invented around 1750, inspired by Japanese paper-making.

Squash & Sweet Potato Purée in a Zucchini Pot

Serves 3

1 medium to large zucchini

4 ounces winter squash like acorn or butternut

4 ounces sweet potato

1 tablespoon EVOO

Pinch of sea salt

1 tablespoon maple syrup (optional)

¾ teaspoon ground cinnamon

This container may look like a mini flowerpot, but it is actually a sliver of zucchini grilled and rolled to form a vessel. The zucchini vessel holds a purée of winter squash and sweet potato. Aside from its charm, there is something wholly satisfying about a dish with an edible container, particularly when the container and its contents are different varieties of the same species.

30 minutes

Boil, pan-grill

Fruit

Corn on the cob, oatmeal, chapati or laffa

Make the purée (steps 1–3) the day or night before. Reheat it gently in a small pot with 3 tablespoons boiling hot water.

1. Peel the squash and sweet potato. Cut each into inch-square cubes. Note: you could use just squash or only sweet potato for a similarly sweet result.

2. Place in a medium-sized pot and cover with water.

3. Bring to a boil; cover and simmer for about 15–20 minutes, or until the squash and sweet potato are soft. Drain most of the water from the pot, leaving about a quarter-inch. Add the maple syrup if desired. Use an immersion blender to purée the squash and sweet potato together until the consistency is smooth but not too watery. Allow to cool a bit.

4. Wash the zucchini by immersing it in water. Slice it lengthwise into 1/2 inch-thick strips. Use a pastry brush to rub olive oil onto one side of each strip.

5. Heat a cast iron or stainless steel skillet for about 20 seconds. Add as many of the strips as will fit flat in the pan, olive-oil-brushed side down. While one side is cooking, brush the other side with the remaining olive oil.

6. Turn the strips over when they turn a golden brown. Cook the second side until it is the same golden brown. Remove from pan and dredge on a brown paper bag.

(continued)

squash S

7. Roll each zucchini strip to form a cylinder-shaped basket; place each one on a plate.

8. Spoon the squash-sweet-potato purée into the center of the zucchini basket.

9. Sprinkle with cinnamon (about ¼ teaspoon for each basket) and serve.

Squash is rich in dietary fiber and in vitamins A, C and B6. It contains potassium, manganese and iron too.

All squash varieties belong to the cucurbit family. Summer squash (zucchini and yellow squash) is thin-skinned and sometimes eaten raw, while winter squash varieties are harvested and eaten when the seeds are fully mature and the skin has hardened into a tough, protective rind. These varieties store well for winter use, and they are always cooked.

Inspired by the protective skin of a winter squash or an orange and expedited by climate change awareness, edible packaging may be the future food wrapping. Sorghum spoons and mushroom packaging materials are now widely available. Stay tuned.

S squash

Pair the vegetable dishes in this book with complementary grain recipes to make each breakfast seasonal, balanced, sustaining and delicious.

Serves 2

A few slices of your favorite unyeasted whole grain bread; you may also use pita.

Note: steamed bread works well for bread that is 3 or more days old.

A chewier, more digestible bread adaptation that ramps up the taste, moistens and softens the texture.

3 minutes

Steam

Cauliflower Rice with Corn; Dressed with Cress; Endive Fatoush; Fatoush!; Italian Parsley Edamame Hummus; Rainbow Matchstick Salad; Squash & Sweet Potato Purée in a Zucchini Pot; Water-Sautéed Mustard Greens with Sumac.

1. Fill a steamer pot with 1–2 inches of water. Cover and bring to a boil.

2. Place bread in steamer basket and put basket into steamer pot. Cover with lid.

3. Steam for about 60–90 seconds. Remove from steamer basket. Bread should be soft, moist and fragrant. Enjoy with nut butter, hummus or another spread.

Fatoush!

Serves 4–5

3–4 curly green lettuce leaves
3–4 tatsoi leaves
3–4 mizuna leaves
A few sprigs dill
A few sprigs oregano
1–2 chives, with flowers
Sprig lemon mint
Sprig spearmint
⅓ cup raw walnuts
½ to 1 lemon
Fine sea salt to taste

Just as Aristotle reminded us that the whole is greater than the sum of its parts, so is a fatoush. The beauty of this Arabic salad of finely chopped greens and herbs is also its bane: the tiny fragments of greens and herbs lose their distinct flavor while they contribute to the overall essence of the dish. Greens that may be too bitter to eat alone become sweet and fragrant when chopped and integrated into this salad.

A fatoush is a metaphor for community and a perfect breakfast cue: venture out into the new day as a team player because, yes, the whole is more powerful and more prone to greatness than each of its parts.

| 12 minutes | Raw | Leaf | Ojiya, pancakes, polenta, steamed bread |

1. Wash all the greens together by immersing them in a large bowl of water. Let the greens dry in a colander or wire mesh basket.

2. In the meantime, heat a stainless steel or cast iron skillet on a medium flame for about 45 seconds. Add the whole walnuts. Allow them to heat on all sides by turning them constantly. When a pleasant, nutty smell infuses the air and the walnuts turn a golden brown, remove them from the pan. When they are cool, chop them into tiny pieces.

3. Separate each leafy green and herb. Chop each leafy green and herb separately, one by one, into tiny pieces and place in a medium-sized mixing bowl.

4. Add the toasted walnuts and sprinkle a pinch or two of fine sea salt on the greens. Toss all ingredients together.

5. Squeeze the lemon and pour onto the salad; mix in well. Garnish with the whole edible purple chive flower or pull the petals apart and integrate with the salad (above right). Serve.

Another brassica (cousin of cabbage and mustard), tatsoi is a bok choy variety known by many other names including Chinese flat cabbage, rosette pakchoi, broad-beaked mustard, spoon mustard or spinach mustard. It has a soft, creamy texture and more subtle flavor than its mustard relations.

Tatsoi's dark color reflects a dense concentration of vitamins and minerals that include vitamins C and A, carotenoids, folic acid, calcium, potassium and iron.

Considered native to China, tatsoi has also been used in Japanese cuisine for thousands of years and is a venerated ancient green.

t

tatsoi

Dressed with Cress

Serves 4–6 adapted from
Joan Nathan

½ pound Portobello mushrooms,
sliced into fine slivers

1 medium-sized onion, sliced
into half-moons

3 tablespoons EVOO

1 cup walnuts, almonds
or pecans

Sea salt and freshly ground
pepper, to taste

1 small bunch of upland cress

Sourdough baguette and
celery boats for serving

Whether you call it upland cress, garden pepper cress, mustard and cress, pepperwort, pepper grass or poor man's pepper, these greens have a peppery, tangy flavor and are packed with nutrients. Here they provide perfect balance by lightening and freshening up the meaty vegan chopped liver spread. The meatiness is courtesy of the powerful portobello mushrooms. Eat this protein-rich dish for breakfast and watch that mid-morning snack craving evaporate.

| 40 minutes (or 5 minutes if you pre-make chopped liver) | Raw | Leaf, stem | Steamed sourdough bread |

 Make the chopped "liver" spread the night before and refrigerate. This will save you about a half hour so the dish will take less than five minutes to prepare in the morning.

1. Place the nuts in a skillet and dry-roast them, turning them so all sides of the nuts are exposed to the heat. Allow them to cool and then roughly chop them into small pieces.

2. Rinse the mushrooms. Slice them lengthwise into slivers and set aside.

3. Slice the onion into half-moons.

4. Heat a medium-sized stainless steel or cast iron skillet over a medium flame until the pan is very warm. Do not use Teflon or any other treated material. Add the EVOO and swirl it around so it covers the bottom of the pan. Place the sliced onion in the pan and sauté until it begins to wilt, sweat and become translucent – about 4 minutes. Add a pinch of coarse sea salt.

5. Add the sliced mushrooms and sauté together with the onions until both are soft and lightly browned, about 15–20 minutes in all. Sprinkle more sea salt and black pepper to taste.

6. Turn into a blender or food processor; add the nuts, a bit more salt and pepper if needed, and a tablespoon of water.

7. Spread in celery boats or on a piece of steamed whole-grain sourdough bread (see recipe on p. 77) and top with fresh upland cress.

Upland cress usually grows in dirt. This distinguishes it from watercress that grows in water. It can be eaten raw or cooked, but the nutrients are more potent when raw.

One serving of upland cress supplies 516% of the daily vitamin K requirement, 83% of C and 43% of A. High in manganese, iron, magnesium and calcium, it also provides protein.

Indian upland cress is called chandrashoor. Its seeds, halloon, are used in Ayurvedic medicine as an antibacterial, appetite stimulant, diuretic, digestive aid and to treat liver disorders and scurvy.

Dolmades!

Makes about 25 stuffed grape leaves

¼ cup pine nuts

¾ cup long grain white rice

1 small onion, minced

¼ cup EVOO

¼ cup fresh dill, chopped

⅛ cup fresh mint, chopped

3 tablespoons freshly squeezed lemon juice

½ tablespoon lemon zest

1 cup vegetable broth

25 large grape leaves (fresh or jarred)

Fine sea salt and fresh-ground pepper to taste

1 tablespoon coarse sea salt (for boiling the grape leaves)

Dolmades is Greek for stuffed grape leaves. All the food groups are represented in this vegan version: grain (rice), vegetables (grape leaf and onion), protein (pine nuts), fruit (lemon) and spices (herbs). The result? A neat, portable meal. Keyword is portable, not fast! I suggest you make a large batch of these when you have a free afternoon. Freeze some, put the others in the fridge and eat them for breakfast at room temperature over the course of a few days.

2 hours   Boil   Leaf   Lemon wedges, raw radishes, yogurt or goatgurt

1. If you are picking and using fresh grape leaves, choose younger leaves that are as large and wide as possible.

2. Use a stainless steel or cast iron skillet to toast the pine nuts on a medium flame. Use cooking chopsticks to turn the nuts, until they begin to sweat and turn a light golden brown. Remove from the pan.

3. Heat a medium-sized heavy pot on a medium flame for about 30 seconds. Add half of the olive oil and warm it for about 20 seconds.

4. Add the minced onion and sauté until it softens and becomes translucent. Add the rice and stir well until it is integrated with the onion, sautéeing the two together for another minute or two. Pour in a half cup of the warm vegetable broth and lower the flame. Simmer the rice, onions and broth uncovered for about 10 minutes until all the liquid is absorbed and the rice is al dente, partially cooked. Do not cook the rice completely or the grape leaves will be mushy. Remove the pot from the flame.

5. Add the chopped dill, mint, pine nuts, 1½ tablespoons of the lemon juice and the lemon zest to the pot. Season with sea salt and pepper and stir well. Allow the rice mixture to cool to room temperature.

6. If using fresh grape leaves, fill a large pot with water, add a few pinches of coarse sea salt and bring to a boil. Trim any long stems from the grape leaves. Place the leaves in the water (about two at a time) and let them boil for about 3 minutes, until they are soft and more pliable. Remove them with a wire mesh skimmer and place them in cold water. Remove leaves from the water and pat dry. Or, use ready-to-roll cured grape leaves from a jar.

(continued)

vine leaves

7. Stuff and roll the grape leaves. If you find any grape leaves with holes, set them aside to line the pan you'll use to cook the stuffed leaves. Place a leaf on a flat surface with the shiny (smooth) side down, veiny or textured side up. Place about 2 tablespoons of the rice filling at the base end of the leaf where the stem was. Fold this base end of the leaf over the filling and seal it by pressing it. Fold the left and right sides of the leaf inward over the leaf to cover the filling. Now continue rolling the leaf (without squeezing too hard, as the rice needs space to expand when cooked) until it forms a neat oblong cylinder. Seal it gently. Repeat until all the leaves are stuffed.

8. Line a large, deep skillet with any damaged leaves, creating a bed. Place all the stuffed leaves in the pan, layering and packing them tightly. This helps keep the leaves whole as they cook.

9. Add the remaining vegetable broth, olive oil, lemon juice and the stuffed leaves. Gently heat the pan to a simmer; then lower the heat so the leaves cook slowly. Place an inverted heat-safe plate on top of the stuffed leaves as a weight to keep them in place. Cover the pot and let the dolmades cook for 30–40 minutes. When they are tender, they are ready.

10. Serve them warm or cold with olives, radish wheels, lemon wedges, plain yogurt or goatgurt.

Stuffed grape leaves are a staple in the cuisines of Afghanistan, Armenia, Bulgaria, Greece, Iran, Israel, Lebanon, Pakistan, Romania, Turkey and Vietnam.

Grape leaves provide fiber, vitamins A and K, calcium and iron. In traditional folk medicine, grape leaves were used to stop bleeding, inflammation and pain.

V

vine leaves

Pay it forward

Eating vegetables for breakfast is a win-win. A boon for the body, it also helps sustain the planet, adding oxygen to the atmosphere, eliminating waste and toxins. Here are some ways to use vegetables and herbs that reach beyond the kitchen.

SOUND

Founded in 1998, the 11-member Vienna Vegetable Orchestra explores the acoustic qualities of veggies using carrot clarinets, flutes and recorders, leek violins and pumpkin drums. Their repertoire includes titles like *Beet-L*, *Bumpkins*, *Nightshades* and *Greenhouse*.
vegetableorchestra.org

BANDAGE

Nori (used for wrapping sushi and in the recipe on p. 72) is a custom-sizable band-aid for basic cuts. The trace minerals and iron help stop the bleeding, it has antifungal properties, and you can wrap it tight without additional adhesive. It comes off painlessly and is compostable. Note: don't use salted or seasoned nori strips.

REPLANT

Replant your kitchen scraps and watch them regrow. Best veggies to regrow in dirt are all lettuces, garlic (plant a clove and you'll get a bulb) and ginger root (soak first). Replant carrots, scallions and celery in water.

WRAP

Use basil, mint, scallions and edible flowers to wrap a gift. Above, a gift of homemade soup in a thermos is entwined with basil and mint. Unwrap the gift and use the herbs to garnish the soup.

A favorite veggie gift: a bouquet of hydroponically grown lettuces.

SCULPT

Since 1897, there has been an annual competition in Oaxaca, Mexico on December 23rd called the Night of the Radishes (*Noche de Rabanos*). Oversized radishes are carved into human, animal and inanimate shapes creating ravishing, radical radish scenes.

BOOKMARK

Sometimes veggies are wrapped with a plastic tab. You won't find them wrapped this way at farmer's markets—yet another reason to shop there. Wait: don't trash them just yet. These plastic tabs double as bookmarks.

Rainbow Matchstick Salad

Serves 4

1 watermelon radish
1 yellow carrot, with top
1 purple carrot, with top
1 orange carrot, with top
1 blood orange
1 lime
Sea salt flakes

Everyone loves a rainbow. It is a symbol of diversity, wholeness and solidarity. A rainbow is a testament to how much each slightly different part contributes to the whole.

I am a big fan of watermelon radishes and rainbow carrots. In addition to their obvious eye candy edge, each different shade of root vegetable provides marginally different health benefits. This punchy salad is bursting with color, energy, nutrients and, best of all, crunch.

20 minutes

Raw

Root, leaf

Steamed bread, couscous, risotto

Wash and slice the night or day before. Store the cut vegetables in cold water in the fridge. Assemble in the morning. Or assemble the salad the night before and dress with lime juice in the morning.

1. Peel and wash the radish. Slice it in half lengthwise, then cut into ⅛-inch-thick half moons. Slice the half moons lengthwise into 3-inch-long matchstick shapes.

2. Cut the leafy green tops off the carrots. Discard about three-quarters, wash the remaining quarter and chop them roughly. Scrape any tiny white hairs and rough spots from the skin of each carrot. Wash them.

3. Slice each carrot into ⅛-inch thick ovals by cutting on the diagonal. Cut each oval lengthwise into about 6–7 matchsticks.

4. Build each salad on a separate plate by layering the orange, yellow and purple carrot sticks and topping with the pink watermelon radish. Save a few sticks of each color for the top. Garnish with chopped green carrot tops. Sprinkle sea salt flakes on top.

5. Cut the blood orange in half. Cut each half into 3–4 sections. Peel and scatter around the edges of the salad. Squeeze lime juice on top of each salad to taste. Serve.

watermelon radish

Hundreds of radish types come in pink, red, purple, green, black and white. The watermelon radish is an heirloom Chinese variety with creamy white skin on the outside. Its bright pinkish-red inside flesh is revealed only upon slicing. It ranges in size from small-as-a-golf-ball to big-as-a-softball.

Remember the long-haired fairy tale heroine Rapunzel? She was named after a particular radish that her mother craved in pregnancy. In an effort to satisfy his wife's rapunzel radish craving, her husband stole some from a neighbor's garden and got caught red-handed (literally). The consequence? He had to hand over his baby daughter to the witch.

Winter Squash Nishime

Serves 2–3

Half a kabocha (aka buttercup) squash

1 leek

5 celery stalks

1 inch-square piece of kombu (aka kelp)

1 tablespoon aged soy sauce

3–4 dandelion, kale or watercress leaves

Dubbed "waterless cooking," nishime is a traditional Japanese method of long-steaming vegetables with very little water and a small piece of kelp (kombu). The dish is warming and strengthening, both especially desirable in cool weather. And did I say sweet?

40 minutes

Long-steam

Fruit

Millet mash, rice, oat or barley porridge

 You may cook this dish the day before. In the morning, remove from fridge and eat at room temperature. Or, place a scant ¼ cup of water in a small lidded pot, add desired portion of nishime, and reheat gently (on a low flame). Ready in 4–5 minutes.

1. Wash the celery stalks well. Cut the leek in half and wash each half with care. Rinse the skin of the kabocha squash.

2. Place about ½ inch of water in the bottom of a small to medium-sized heavy-lidded pot. Add the kombu.

3. Cut the leek into 3-inch-long spears.

4. Clean and then cut the celery into similarly sized 3-inch-long pieces.

5. Remove the seeds from the squash. Cut the kabocha squash into thin wedges. You will have about 5–7 pieces.

6. Place the leek pieces in the pot, arranging them over the kombu. Layer the celery over the leeks in the pot. Place the squash on top of the celery, fitting the pieces in snugly. Cover the pot and cook on a medium flame.

7. While the nishime cooks, wash the dandelion, kale or watercress. If using kale, remove the tough end of the spine. Chop and set aside.

8. When you see the steam rise from the pot lid, lower the flame and simmer, covered, for about 25–40 minutes, until the vegetables are soft. Drizzle the soy sauce evenly.

(continued)

winter squash

9. Cover the pot again. Shake the pot and all of its ingredients firmly and briefly. Cook on a very low flame for another 5–10 minutes. Remove from the heat and arrange the vegetables in individual bowls.

10. Sprinkle the chopped raw dandelion, kale or watercress on top of the veggies. The greens will wilt slightly from the heat. Serve.

Acorn. Banana. Butternut. Buttercup. Carnival. Delicata. Dumpling. Fairytale pumpkin. Gem. Gold nugget. Hubbard. Kabocha. Lakota. Red kuri. Spaghetti. Turban. These are some of the more common of the hundred varieties of edible winter squash, which come in all sizes and shapes. Some of the most intricately shaped winter squash are inedible gourds.

A member of the cucurbit family—a trailing, climbing genus that includes cucumbers and melons—winter squash is picked at full maturity. Also known nonspecifically as pumpkins, they have thick skin with firm, flavorful warm-colored flesh and big edible seeds. They take at least three months to mature, while summer squash takes about 40 days.

Low in calories, high in dietary fiber and complex carbohydrates, winter squash is super-rich in vitamin A, potassium and folate. It also provides B vitamins, iron and omega-3 fatty acids.

Pair the vegetable dishes in this book with complementary grain recipes to make each breakfast seasonal, balanced, sustaining and delicious.

Serves 4–6

1 tablespoon extra virgin olive oil

2 cloves garlic, minced

4–5 medium-sized ramps (or scallions), chopped

1½ cups hulled barley

4 cups vegetable stock, heated

1 cup peas, fresh or frozen

Salt and pepper

½ teaspoon saffron threads

Ground pistachio or cashews, to taste
or
Grated Romano or Parmigiano cheese, to taste

You can make this the night or day before. Refrigerate overnight. Put about ⅙ cup vegetable stock in a pot, add the cooked risotto. Reheat gently over a small flame for about 5–8 minutes and serve.

A chewy riff on this classic flavorful Italian rice dish.

55 minutes

Sauté, boil, simmer

Asparagus Almondine; Carrot Flowers; Cauliflower Rice with Corn; Parsnip Curls; Purple Daikon Corn Salad; Rainbow Matchstick Salad

1. Use a deep stainless-steel skillet to sauté the ramps and garlic in olive oil until softened. Add the barley and cook for 5 minutes until it is lightly toasted and you can smell its nutty flavor.

2. Add 3 cups of the stock, salt and pepper. Bring to a boil, cover and simmer about 25 minutes, stirring occasionally and adding stock as needed.

3. Add the saffron, with some additional broth if needed. Simmer an additional 10–15 minutes.

4. Stir in the peas, some of the nuts or cheese and more salt and pepper to taste. Cook for 2–3 minutes more, making sure the peas remain bright green.

5. Serve hot, with fresh ground nuts or grated cheese on the side.

Spinach Rolls with Xigua Tops

Serves 2–4

1 thick carrot

1 bunch of spinach

Quarter or sixth of a watermelon, depending on size

½ lime (optional)

Xigua is the Chinese name for the African fruit we call watermelon. It is a fruit, not a vegetable, and a key ingredient in this largely vegetable dish because it is refreshing, hydrating, crispy and sweet. Perched on top of a roll-up made of carrot, a root, filled with spinach, a leaf, xigua grows on a vine and rests atop the soil, er, dirt. It balances the dish, energetically, texturally and visually.

12 minutes

Raw

Fleshy fruit, rind

Corn on the cob or fried polenta

Steam the spinach the night before (steps 1–2) and you may roll them up too (step 5).

xigua

1. Wash the spinach well and trim any long stems. Place the clean spinach in a bamboo or stainless steel steamer basket.

2. Pour about 2 inches of water into the steamer pot, cover the pot and bring water to a boil. Place the steamer basket of spinach in the pot and cover. When the spinach wilts but still retains its deep green hue (this should take about 1 minute), remove the steamer basket from the pot and turn off the flame. Set spinach aside to cool.

3. Peel the carrot. Remove the outermost layer of skin. Continue to peel the carrot on the same side—so you will get wide ribbons. Set aside about 8 carrot ribbons.

4. Cut a slice of watermelon. Cut the piece into small strips and cut them into tiny rectangles about 1 inch long by ½ inch wide.Assemble the roll-ups

5. Take 4 or 5 of the cooled spinach leaves. Roll them up, squeezing out any excess water.

6. Fold in the ends to create a small log with a flat bottom. It should stand up on a flat surface and be about 1½ inches high.

(continued)

7. Wrap one ribbon of carrot peel around the spinach log. The peel will be long enough to wrap around the spinach twice or more. Gently press the end into the already-wrapped peel; it should stick.

8. Top with a small rectangle of watermelon. Squeeze fresh lime juice on top, if desired.

 xigua

Originally from Africa, watermelon is a tropical or subtropical member of the cucurbit family, along with cucumber and squash. It has a thick rind that contains the amino acid citrulline and is often eaten pickled. Botanically, watermelon is a pepo, a modified berry. If that's a surprise, there's more: other unexpected berries include banana, olive, tomato, potato and zucchini.

Xigua is 91 percent water and rich in vitamin C, with some vitamin A. The pulp is rich in lycopene, a carotenoid antioxidant that prevents heart disease, hardening of the arteries and some cancers.

In the southern Japanese city of Zentsuji, farmers developed a way to save space by growing watermelons in metal and glass boxes so they would assume the shape of their container and be stackable. They come in square, rectangular and pyramid shapes, packaged in handcrafted boxes and priced at several times the classic egg-shaped melons.

Pair the vegetable dishes in this book with complementary grain recipes to make each breakfast seasonal, balanced, sustaining and delicious.

Serves 6

1 cup organic medium or coarse cornmeal (aka polenta or grits)

1 teaspoon sea salt, or to taste

2 basil leaves

½ teaspoon tekka powder (optional)

A soft, creamy Italian comfort food dish (aka grits in the U.S.) that is gluten-free, fibrous and protein-rich.

55 minutes | Boil, simmer | Carrot Flowers; Fatoush!; Kale, Chopped!; The Orange & the Green (Bean); Parsnip Curls; Steamed Radish Roots & Greens; Spinach Rolls with Xigua Tops

 If you want to eat soft polenta (porridge) in the morning, you must make it in the morning. You can make soft polenta for dinner the night before (steps 1–3) and let it set overnight. Fry it in the morning (step 4).

1. Pour 5 cups of water into a medium-sized pot. Add a pinch of sea salt and bring to a boil. Now pour the cornmeal SLOWLY into the boiling water, whisking as it hits the water to avoid clumping. (I am right-handed so I use my left hand to pour the cornmeal and my right hand to whisk.)

2. These moments are key to achieving a truly creamy, clumpless polenta. Once you have added the whole cup of cornmeal, use a wooden spoon to mix it. The polenta will begin to bubble occasionally. Cook it, uncovered or partially covered, for about 45 minutes, periodically scraping the pot's bottom with the wooden spoon to prevent sticking.

3. If the polenta begins to get dry, you may have to add a bit of boiling water. Do so, as needed. The consistency should be soft and creamy but not watery. When it reaches this texture and smells sweet, ladle into a bowl. Garnish with a basil or parsley leaf and sprinkle some tekka powder on top, if desired. *Tekka is a Japanese condiment made by slow-cooking miso and root vegetables together for over 16 hours. Its rich mineral content helps strengthen the blood. Polenta is often served with melted cheese; this is a flavorful, delicious alternative.*

4. Pour the remaining polenta into a deep glass dish (a small Pyrex will do) and allow it to set. When it cools, place in the refrigerator. Cut it into 2–3-inch square or rectangular pieces and fry in olive oil another day. Garnish with carrots, herbs and tekka powder.

Yams 'n Sprouts

Serves 4

2 cups baby Brussels sprouts
One garnet yam
1 tablespoon EVOO
A *few* pinches sea salt

Sweet potato or yam, that is the question. While both may be orange-ish starchy tubers, neither is a potato, and botanically they are very different. These garnet yams are red-skinned and orange-fleshed, yet most yams are white-fleshed and cylindrical with dry, scaly skin; sweet potatoes are sweeter and more moist, with tapered ends. Either would work well in this dish. Yams and Brussels sprouts may seem like an unlikely couple, but actually the dish is balanced (a tuber and a round veggie) in a stick-to-the-ribs kind of way. Teamed up with a whole grain, this is a breakfast for champions.

25 minutes

Sauté

Tuber

Couscous, oatmeal, ojiya, wild rice

Cook this dish (steps 1–4) about 90%, and reheat in the pan.

1. Wash the Brussels sprouts well by immersing them in water. Remove any dark spots at the base and any yellowed or brown outer leaves.

2. Peel the yam. Slice it into rounds and then cut the rounds into quarter-inch squares.

3. Heat a cast iron or stainless steel skillet on a medium flame for about one minute. It should be very hot. Add the olive oil and then the Brussels sprouts.

4. Use a wooden spoon to turn them, exposing all sides to the heat. After a few minutes, when they begin to brown, add a few pinches of sea salt; then add the yam squares. Cover the yam pieces with the Brussels sprouts, exposing the yams to the pan's heat. When the yams brown (this should take about 4–5 minutes), remove from pan and serve.

yam

The more nutrient-rich sweet potato belongs to the morning glory family, while the yam is a member of the Dioscoraceas, a group of tropical and subtropical herbs and shrubs. There are over 200 varieties of yams, not all edible, and some of them toxic. Containing potassium, manganese, vitamins B6 and C, some wild yams contain phytochemicals that increase estrogen in the body.

Native to West Africa, they are used in African, Caribbean, Indian, Japanese and Latino cuisine. In parts of West Africa, yams are considered sacred and are used in rituals celebrating birth, death, marriage and recovery from accidents and disease. Yams can grow up to 5 feet long and weigh as much as 150 pounds.

Zinguini!

Serves 4

2 medium to large zucchini
1½ tablespoons EVOO
1 teaspoon tekka powder

Zoodles (zucchini noodles), have become a go-to gluten-free pasta sub. Zinguini is a portmanteau (compound) of zucchini and linguini. Zoodles are round while zinguini are flat. You need a spiralizer to make a substantial quantity of zoodles, while you need only a knife to score these flat-shaped zucchini-that-resemble-linguini. Tools aside, you'll want to eat oodles!

10 minutes   Quick-sauté   Fruit and flower   Linguini pasta

1. Wash the zucchini well. Remove tough stem and bottom; leave the skin on. Slice each zucchini lengthwise, into about 5 or 6 quarter-inch-wide slabs. Cut each slab into several skinny linguine-like strips (about 7–9 strips per slab).

2. Heat a stainless steel or cast iron skillet on a medium flame for about one minute. Add the olive oil and heat it for about 40 seconds. Place the zucchini strips in the pan, turning them until they become a light golden brown on all sides. This should take a few minutes.

3. Remove from the pan and arrange on individual plates. Sprinkle about ¼ teaspoon of tekka powder on each portion and serve.

zucchini

Zucchini is the Italian word for "little pumpkins" because these cucurbits are, in fact, immature squash or pumpkins containing soft, edible seeds. High in folate, potassium and vitamin A, zucchini is low in calories and is a boon to weight loss.

Native to Mexico, zucchini is another of Christopher Columbus' discoveries. He brought them back to Italy where they became popular generations later. The Italians introduced them to the French, who called them "courgettes." Eventually they made their way to the British Isles, where they became known as "marrows."

RECIPE ▼ GO–WITH ▶	Barley Risotto	Millet Mash	Ojiya
Asparagus Almondine	✳		
Sweet Beet			
Spicy Brussels Sprouts			✳ ✳
Carrot Flowers	✳ ✳ ✳	✳ ✳ ✳	
Cauliflower Rice	✳ ✳		
Purple Daikon Salad	✳ ✳		
Endive Fatoush		✳ ✳ ✳	
Fennel, Daikon & Shitake Nishime		✳ ✳ ✳	
The Orange & the Green (Bean)			
Green Sashimi			
Italian Parsley Edamame Hummus			
Jerusalem Artichoke Pancakes			
Kale, Chopped			
Green Pinwheels			
Water-Sautéed Mustard Greens			
Napa Cabbage Roll-ups			✳ ✳
Onions & Shitake on a Tofu Pad			
Parsnip Curls	✳	✳	✳
Quinoa Tabouleh			
Steamed Radish Roots & Greens			✳ ✳ ✳ ✳
Baga Chips			✳ ✳
Yellow Carrot Nori Rolls			
Squash & Sweet Potato Purée			
Fatoush			✳ ✳ ✳
Dressed with Cress			
Dolmades			
Rainbow Matchstick Salad			
Winter Squash Nishime		✳ ✳	
Spinach Rolls with Xigua Tops			
Yams 'n Sprouts			✳ ✳
Zinguini			

Polenta	Rice	Steamed Bread	Other
	❄		Quinoa
	🍁 ❄		Couscous
	❄ 🍁		Oatmeal
☀ 🍁 ❄			
		🍁 ❄	Couscous
			Barley salad
		☀ ❄ 🍁	
	🍁 ❄ ❄		
❄ 🍁 ❄ ☀			Oatmeal
	🍁 ❄ ☀ ❄		
		❄ ☀ 🍁 ❄	Corn or rice cakes
			Pickle, sauerkraut
☀ 🍁 ❄			Corn on the cob
			Pickle
	☀ ❄ 🍁 ❄	☀ ❄ 🍁 ❄	
	🍁 ☀		
	❄ 🍁		
❄			
			Greens
❄ ☀ 🍁 ❄	❄ ☀ 🍁 ❄		Pancakes
	🍁 ❄		Oatmeal
	☀ ❄ 🍁		
		🍁 ❄	Corn on the cob
☀ 🍁 ❄		☀ 🍁 ❄	Pancakes
		🍁 ❄ ❄ ☀	
			Radish, goatgurt
	🍁 ☀ ❄	🍁 ☀ ❄	Couscous
	❄ 🍁		Barley or oat porridge
☀ 🍁			Corn on the cob
	❄ 🍁		Couscous, oatmeal
			Linguini pasta

You can use these pages to keep a Breakfast Diary, entering the date and full breakfast menu.
You may include comments on how you felt after eating it.

DATE	BREAKFAST MENU	NOTES

DATE	BREAKFAST MENU	NOTES

You can use these pages to make notes on the recipes you've made in this book. Note what worked well and what needs tweaking.

DATE	RECIPE	KEEP	TWEAK

DATE	RECIPE	KEEP | TWEAK

This book would not exist without the help and support of so many big-hearted people. For planting the seeds for this book I am grateful to my teachers Denny Waxman and Michelle Nemer, as well as all my students and clients who teach and inspire me daily. To every cook who has invited me into their kitchen and shared their knowledge and recipes, thank you. For helping me to grow and birth this book I am deeply grateful to Oded Halahmy for his most generous support, patience and guidance, to Luke Peterson for making it happen, and to Malka Percal for her impeccable editing and confidence in me. For her inimitable acumen and eye, I thank Alice Gottesman. For nourishment and care I thank Sigal Greenberg for her attentive, mindful encouragement, Joan Downs, whose discernment and support are invaluable, all of my blog followers and readers, and my family and friends who come to my table with open, discriminating palates. My mother's lifelong unconditional support and cheerleading extended passionately to *Vegetables for Breakfast* as did my father's as he continued to joke about it while nibbling on a carrot some mornings. I am grateful to my husband David for his patience and support and to my precious daughters, Elsie and Ma'yan, who never once hesitated to admit to consuming broccoli, cabbage and even collard greens for breakfast.

BOOKS CONSULTED AND RECOMMENDED

Belleme, John & Jan, *Japanese Foods That Heal*, Tuttle, 2007.

Enders, Giulia, *GUT The Inside Story of Our Body's Most Underrated Organ*, Greystone Books, 2015.

Green, Aliza, *Field Guide to Produce*, Quirk Productions, 2004.

Root, Waverly, *Food*, Fireside, 1980.

Rupp, Rebecca, *How Carrots Won the Trojan War*, Storey, 2011.

Waters, Alice, *Chez Panisse Vegetables*, Harper Collins, 1996.

INGREDIENTS

Brown mustard seeds
kalustyans.com

Grape leaves
instacart.com
amazon.com

Pomegranate Molasses and other Middle Eastern products
sadaf.com

Salts and Spices in general
kalustyans.com

Sea Vegetables
Maine Coast Sea Vegetables
seaveg.com

Maine Seaweed
theseaweedman.com

Natural Import Company
naturaimport.com

Tekka and other Japanese condiments
naturalimport.com

ONLINE RESOURCES

The Vegetable Orchestra
vegetableorchestra.org

Virtual World Carrot Museum
carrotmuseum.org

TOOLS

Bamboo Cooking Chopsticks
amazon.com
naturalimport.com

Carrot/Cucumber Peeler and Sharpener (aka Karoto Peeler)
dinointhebox.com
thechefsnook.com

Chef 'n VeggiChop
bedbathandbeyond.com
bloomingdales.com

OXO Good Grips 3 Blade tabletop spiralizer
amazon.com

INDEX

RECIPES BY VEGETABLE

INDEX